Gallery of American Quilts

BOOK 4

American Quilter's Society

P. O. Box 3290 • Paducah, KY 42002-3290

Notice

The quilts in this book are no longer for sale. They were offered by members of the American Quilters's Society in 1992 and 1993.

1011291

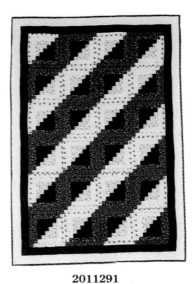

2011291

3011291

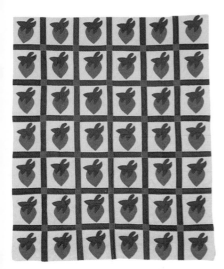

4011291

5011291

6011291

7011291

1011291 – DOUBLE PYRAMID; 84" x 92"; country blue, off-white, burgundy; 100% cotton calicoes & muslin, poly/cotton backing; machine pieced, hand-guided machine quilting; extraloft batting. $431.00

2011291 – LOG CABIN FURROW; 65" x 91"; shades of light & dark browns, off-white lining; cotton/poly blend fabrics, mostly VIP prints; made in Illinois in 1989; machine pieced & quilted; double binding & double stitched. $144.00

3011291 – AUTUMN DEER HUNT; 88" x 104"; brown & beige; machine pieced, hand embroidered & hand quilted; bonded polyester, muslin lining; original leaf embroidery design in autumn colors; made in Missouri in 1990; quilted deer head in brown blocks; ©Ruth Vaughn design. $288.00

4011291 – APPLIQUED STRAWBERRY; 77" x 92"; cream muslin background, strawberry red with white polka dots, green leaves; cotton; hand appliqued with color matched embroidery thread, hand quilted; made in Montana in 1989. $402.00

5011291 – HEARTS & ARROWROOTS; 35" x 35"; ivory, green & burgundy; cotton fabric; made in Minnesota in 1990; hand appliqued & quilted, machine pieced; polyester batting; a ribbon winner in small quilt category at county fair; pattern inspired by Judy Martin's book *Scrapquilts*. $217.00

6011291 – CLIMBING CLEMATIS; 79" x 96"; mauve, shades of green; trellis area is light mauve & off-white narrrow stripes; border is dark green print; cotton & cotton/polyester blend; made in Kansas in 1990; machine pieced, hand quilted with leaves & flower petal designs; mitered borders. $460.00

7011291 – DRESDEN PLATE; 78" x 98"; multicolored with green set with white, white lining; cotton fabric; made in Mississippi in 1990; machine pieced & appliqued, hand quilted; poly fluff batting. $316.00

1021291

2021291

3021291

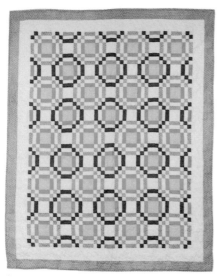

4021291

5021291

6021291

1021291 – TWINKLING STARS; 87" x 102"; aqua, periwinkle blue, purple, fuchsia with hand-dyed pieces in various soft colors; cotton fabrics; machine pieced & machine quilted (in waves pattern); Cotton Classic batting; made in California in 1990; hand-dyed fabrics are marbled & watercolor-like designs. $259.00

2021291 – AS THE CROW FLIES; 56" x 84"; dark green & red, gray, pink, cream; gray pin-dot border, light brown & white print backing; 100% cotton; made in Illinois in 1990; machine pieced, hand quilted; low-loft batting; signed & dated. $345.00

3021291 – LONE STAR; 88" x 88"; pale yellows, peaches, aquas, yellow background; 100% cotton; made in New York in 1987; machine pieced & quilted; polyester High-Loft batting. $288.00

4021291 – IRISH JIG; 84" x 101"; earth tones (brown & gold), cream; cotton/polyester fabrics; machine pieced & quilted; made in Missouri in 1991; polyester batting. $230.00

5021291 – HAPPY DAYS; 68" x 86"; prewashed cotton & poly/cotton fabrics with polyfil batting; lining has sheep printed on it; inspired by maker's 4 grandchildren! $259.00

6021291 – FEATURED STAR; 85" x 96"; navy blue color scheme; cotton/polyester fabrics; made in South Dakota in 1986; machine pieced, hand quilted; medium weighted fiberfil; white backing; scalloped border; sheen shine material used. $460.00

7021291 – VARIABLE STAR; 85" x 100"; Williamsburg green, rose/mauve, parchment background prints; 100% cotton prints, cream solid backing; machine pieced, hand quilted; double bound edge with mitered corners; made in Virginia 1990-1991. $690.00

7021291

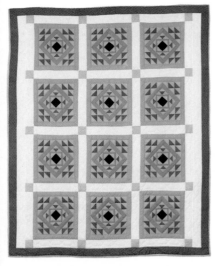

1031291

2031291

3031291

4031291

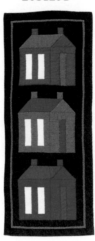

5031291

6031291

7031291

1031291 – SQUARES & TRIANGLES; 82" x 96"; blue with white; cotton/polyester fabric; machine pieced, hand quilted; made in Missouri in 1991; polyester batting. $402.00

2031291 – THREE-IN-ONE WALLHANGINGS; these three wallhangings are to be sold as a unit. The sizes are 11" x 14", 22" x 22" & 30" x 38"; they're entitled Charm Miniature (48 piece), Blue Batik Elephant and Pink & Blue; 100% cotton; machine pieced, hand quilted, some hand embroidery; all ready for hanging; polyester batting. $575.00

3031291 – WEATHERVANE; 80" x 96"; prints & solids, border solid blue; blocks are filled out with white, backing is white; mostly cotton with some cotton/poly; hand pieced & quilted, made in Arkansas in 1988; polyester batting; diamonds quilted in border. $230.00

4031291 – UNICYCLE; 48" x 48"; red, lavendar with blue-green, white & yellow; cotton; made in Massachusettes in 1987; machine pieced, hand quilted; original design using strip piecing; cotton batting. $402.00

5031291 – UNNAMED; 13" x 31"; teal, burgundy & navy blue houses, black background; 100% cotton; made in North Carolina in 1990; hand pieced, hand quilted (9-10 stitches per inch); poly puff low-loft batting; 1" hanging sleeve; black backing. $70.00

6031291 – GIANT DAHLIA; 88" x 113"; mauve & blue; cotton & cotton/poly blend fabrics; made in Kansas in 1991; polyester batting; hand quilted, machine pieced. $345.00

7031291 – VARIABLE STAR; 84" x 111"; mauve with cream; machine pieced & quilted; cotton/polyester fabric; polyester batting. $230.00

1040991

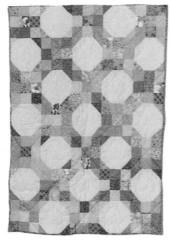

2041291

3041291

4041291

5041291

6041291

1041291 – MARINER'S COMPASS; 90" x 107"; four shades of blue; made in New York in 1990; machine pieced, hand quilted; polyester batting; center compass with four smaller ones on white background; hand quilted by a church group. $402.00

2041291 – SNOWBALL SCRAP; 36" x 50"; pastels & off-white; 100% cotton; made in Wisconsin in 1991; machine pieced & quilted; extra loft polyester batting. $144.00

3041291 – STAR ABLAZE; 88" x 102"; off-white, light cream, beige, rose, mauve, wine–prints & solids; cotton; made in Ohio in 1991; machine pieced; hand quilted both sides of seams of the 648 - 2¼" diamonds in the large star; double fabric bound. $523.00

4041291 – DAISY; 82" x 100"; dusty blue with cream backing; cotton/polyester fabrics; made in South Dakota in 1983; hand appliqued & quilted; fiberfil batting. $431.00

5041291 – GRANDMOTHER'S FAN; 80" x 101"; mauve, cranberry, pink, rose, mint green & evergreen with dusty rose backing; cotton; made by a group in Nebraska in 1991; machine pieced, hand quilted; polyfil batting. $862.00

6041291 – LONE STAR; 45" x 45"; white, Christmas red & green; cotton/polyester blend fabrics; made in 1991 in Kentucky; machine pieced, hand quilted; polyester fiber batting; Lone Star made from bright Christmas prints & solids. $190.00

7041291 – GRANDMOTHER'S FAN; 84" x 98"; blue & pink flowered with unbleached muslin; cotton; made in Mississippi in 1991; machine pieced, hand quilted; polyester batting; off-white cotton backing. $402.00

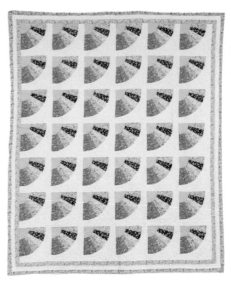

7041291

1051291

2051291

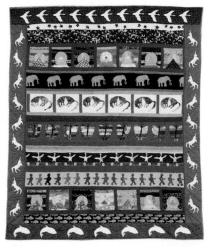

3051291

4051291

5050991

6051291

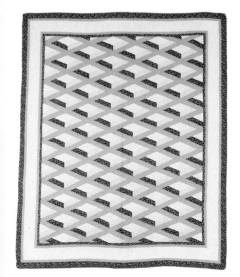

7051291

1051291 – OLD MAID'S PUZZLE; 94" x 94"; pink, brown & muslin; 100% cotton; maker unknown; origin South Carolina; hand pieced & quilted; quilted in feathered circles; one age stain along border, but in good condition for quilt made c. 1860. $230.00

2051291 – PEONY BLUES; 27" x 50"; blue, green, beige background; cotton fabric; made in Minnesota in 1990; hand pieced, quilted & appliqued; polyester batting; sleeve on back for hanging. $132.00

3051291 – UNNAMED; 89" x 100"; multicolored strips of animals & people with a strip of Moon Over the Mountain; cotton fabrics; made in 1984 in Kentucky; hand appliqued & quilted; original pattern. $1150.00

4051291 – ABSTRACT; 75" x 98"; multicolored scrap quilt; machine pieced, hand quilted; cotton fabrics; Mountain Mist batting. $374.00

5051291 – SILHOUETTE; 42" x 55"; off-white (muslin) & black; all cottons; made in Georgia in 1986; hand pieced & quilted; Mountain Mist lite batting; original pattern inspired by cross-stitch; has 1,126 one-inch pieces (squares & strips). $144.00

6051291 – CAROLINA LILY; 82" x 110"; white background with dark forest green stems, leaves & burgundy with shades of mauve for flowers; cotton/polyester fabrics; made in Minnesota in 1987; machine pieced, hand quilted; quilt never used. $546.00

7051291 – SAN MARCO REVISITED IN THE SPRING; 88" x 108"; pale green, pink, black print, off-white, print backing; cottons – back is cotton/polyester blend; made in New Hampshire in 1988 (not used); machine pieced, hand quilted; Mountain Mist batting; this quilt has won awards; the block (large diamond) is a copyrighted design by quiltmaker. $805.00

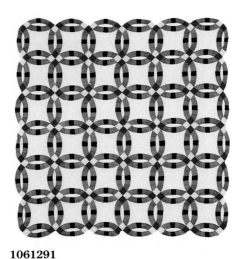

1061291

2061291

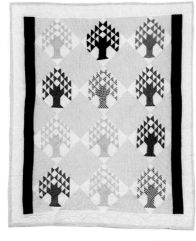

3061291

4061291

5061291

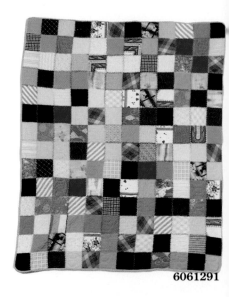

6061291

1061291 – DOUBLE WEDDING RING; 92" x 92"; blue & blue prints on white background with light & dark blue inserts; cotton blends; made in Kentucky in 1990; machine pieced, hand quilted; polyester batting; quilted design in centers plus outline quilting; handmade bias tape. $431.00

2061291 – DRESDEN PLATE; 76" x 101"; peach & white, multicolored plates; cotton/polyester fabrics; made in Tennessee in 1982; hand pieced & quilted; polyester batting. $460.00

3061291 – TREE; 83" x 98"; light green with green flower & white; 100% cotton; made in Georgia in 1989; hand pieced & quilted; polyester batting; backing is cotton muslin. $230.00

4061291 – GEORGETOWN CIRCLES; 84" x 92"; browns-scrap quilt; cotton & cotton blend fabrics; made 1980's in California; hand pieced & quilted; polyester batting; quilt has been shown but never used. $460.00

5061291 – HELTER SKELTER; 69" x 91"; shades of blues from darks to lights, beiges, cranberry red; cotton (sashing & backing are cotton/poly blends); made in Iowa in 1989; machine pieced, hand quilted; many different prints used. $460.00

6061291 – PATCHWORK; 72" x 86"; multicolored polyester fabrics; may be used for bed, wall decor or on a chair; seams embellished with embroidery; polyester batting; made in Kentucky; hand pieced, machine quilted; polyester batting. $172.00

7061291 – JUDY'S STAR; 93" x 108"; rosy pink background, burgundy/burgundy rose print stars; 100% cotton fabrics; made in Louisiana in 1988; machine pieced, hand quilted; the quilt is an adaptation of a Trudie Hughes design; a blue ribbon winner at state fair. $345.00

7061291

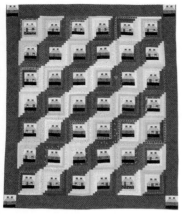

1071291

2071291

3071291

4071291

5071291

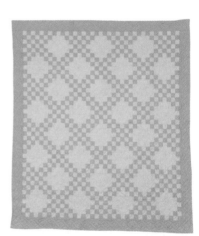

6071291

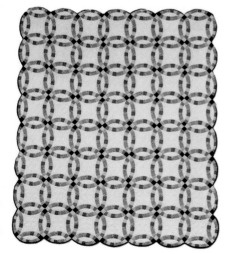

7071291

1071291 – LOG CABIN COTTAGES; 81" x 94"; many different beige & red prints; blue, green & light brown in house block; 100% cotton; made in Maine in 1991; machine pieced, hand quilted; light polyester batting. $345.00

2071291 – GIANT DAHLIA; 86" x 108"; mauves, blues & ecru; cotton blends; made in Wyoming in 1990; machine pieced, hand quilted; polyfil batting; elaborate quilting stitches allow quilt to be reversible; unbleached muslin back. $1,006.00

3071291 – UNNAMED; 86" x 98"; shades of blue with a touch of multiple colors; all cotton top, poly/cotton backing & polyester batting; made in Kansas in 1991; each block trimmed with polyester lace; machine pieced, hand quilted; 1" squares & little boxes quilted in each block. $460.00

4071291 – SPACE FLOWER; 58" x 69"; black, maroon, purple, blue, white – solid colors; cottons & cotton/poly blends, all cotton backing; machine pieced, hand appliqued & quilted; polyfil traditional batting; blue double bias binding. $339.00

5071291 – LOVE RING; 96" x 104"; blue solid & blue print cotton/polyester fabrics; made in Missouri in 1991; machine pieced, hand quilted; polyester batting. $402.00

6071291 – DOUBLE IRISH CHAIN; 80" x 90"; light pink & mint green; 100% cotton; made in Indiana in 1991; machine pieced, hand quilted; polyester batting; tiny tulip prints (large tulip print on backing). $374.00

7071291 – DOUBLE WEDDING RING; 90" x 104"; blue & pink; cotton fabrics; made in Kentucky in 1991; machine pieced, hand quilted; prewashed fabrics; Mountain Mist batting. $374.00

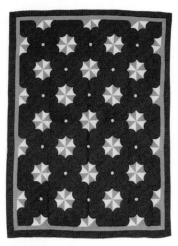

1081291

2081291

3081291

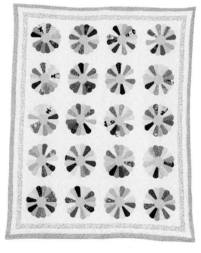

4081291

5081291

6081291

1081291 – DOGWOOD; 78" x 104"; blue with rose, white corners & yellow centers; all cotton front; cotton/poly backing; made in Kansas in 1991; hand quilted, machine pieced yellow centers are appliqued (& padded), mitered corners, double bias binding; polyester batting. $489.00

2081291 – LOG CABIN; 92" x 98"; blue on blue with medium blue lining; made in Alabama in 1990; machine pieced, hand quilted on each side of seam; polyester batting. $402.00

3081291 – STAR; 76" x 92"; each block has an unbleached muslin background with a pink print & yellow print fabric making up stars, the sashing is dark pink; all cotton; blocks made c.1900, quilt put together in 1991 in Kansas; machine pieced, hand quilted with dark pink thread. $345.00

4081291 – DRESDEN PLATE; 75" x 90"; unbleached muslin background, assorted color plates, yellow centers, peach backing; cotton & poly/cotton fabrics; made in Florida in 1991; machine pieced, hand quilted & appliqued; hearts & stripes quilting designs. $345.00

5081291 – LOG CABIN; 81" x 81"; red, white & blue; cotton; made in Arkansas in 1991; machine pieced, hand quilted; polyfil batting, cotton back & binding. $402.00

6081291 – SUNFLOWER; 78" x 90"; yellows shaded, orange, red, browns, & green (leaves & binding), white; cotton & cotton/blends; made in Indiana in 1991; hand appliqued; blue ribbon winner at local fair. $690.00

7081291

7081291 – PREPRINTED DRESDEN PLATE; 91" x 93"; navy blue & maroon-red; cotton & cotton blends; made in Illinois in 1989; machine pieced, hand quilted; preprinted blocks set together with maroon & navy with small dark red flowers coordinating with blocks; prairie points; dark red back quilted with dark red thread. $276.00

1091291

2091291

3091291

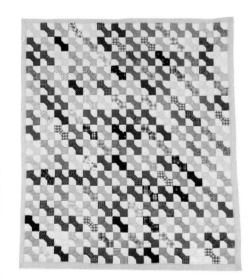

4091291

5091291

6091291

7091291

1091291 – DOUBLE IRISH CHAIN; 86" x 106"; blue & white; cotton fabrics; made in Pennsylvania in 1991; machine pieced & quilted; polyester batting; double binding; feathered wreath in plain squares. $489.00

2091291 – VICTORIAN CRAZY QUILT; 67" x 67"; multicolored scraps & black; silks, satins, velvets & ribbons; history unknown, made in late 1800's in Georgia; large crazy quilt fan blocks combine to give circles, all outlined in feather-stitch embroidery, backing may have been assembled at a later time than the top. $575.00

3091291 – GIANT DAHLIA; 70" x 90"; mountain green, mint, raspberry, mauve, ecru; 100% cotton; made in Nebraska in 1990; machine pieced, hand printed; polyfil batting. $494.00

4091291 – DRESDEN PLATE; 48" x 46"; beige background, plates are greens & pinks (flowered & plain), border is maroon; 100% cotton & muslin; made in Wisconsin in 1991; hand & machine pieced & quilted; polyester batting. $98.00

5091291 – LONE STAR; 80" x 100"; shades of rust, brown, green, gold & orange; off-white background & backing; cotton fabric (diamonds are cotton/poly blend); made in Minnesota in 1989; machine pieced top, small stars are appliqued, hand quilted in the ditch, background has quilted feather circles. $362.00

6091291 – FANS; 84" x 96"; pink & white; 100% cotton; hand & machine pieced, hand quilted; made in Pennsylvania in 1989; polyester batting; quilt has won several awards in local quilt shows. $460.00

7091291 – BOW TIE; 82" x 92"; variety of colors (prints & solids) on white background; cotton & cotton/poly blends; made in Arkansas in 1990; hand pieced & quilted; polyester batting; double bias binding. $259.00

11

1101291

2101291

3101291

4101291

5101291

6101291

1101291 – GIRL BUNNY; 38" x 44"; bunny on pink background, squares are white with pink/green/white print; cotton fabrics; made in North Carolina in 1985 (but unused); machine pieced, hand & machine quilted, machine appliqued; polyester batting. $70.00

2101291 – UNKNOWN; 62" x 87"; orange background, multicolored blocks; cotton; date made is unknown – estimated 1920's, probably in Nebraska; hand pieced & tied (9 times on each 3½" block); floral backing. $288.00

3101291 – CHECKERBOARD GARDEN; 39" x 39"; black, white, lavendar, green with white backing; 100% cotton; made in Virginia in 1991; machine pieced, hand quilted; low loft polyester batting; placement of nine-patch blocks blends diagonally from dark to light; cable quilt design on black border. $230.00

4101291 – UNNAMED STAR; 30" x 30"; brown, pink, green, off-white & blue; 100% cotton; made in Pennsylvania in 1991; machine pieced & quilted; polyfil traditional batting. $45.00

5101291 – FLOWER GARDEN; 84" x 98"; multicolored patterns on the flowers on white background; scalloped edges, white back; 100% cotton top, 50-50 poly/cotton backing; made in Southern Iowa in 1989; machine sewn top with hand quilting on rest of quilt; Mountain Mist batting. $345.00

6101291 – STAR OF THE ORIENT; 45" x 45"; blues with brown, gold & beign accents; cotton & cotton blend fabrics; polyester batting; made in 1987 in California; machine pieced, hand quilted. $172.00

7101291 – MORNING STAR; 84" x 100"; soft pink, blue, rose & brown; 100% cotton; made in Wisconsin in 1991; machine pieced & quilted; polyester batting; quilted with heart motif. $288.00

7101291

12

1111291

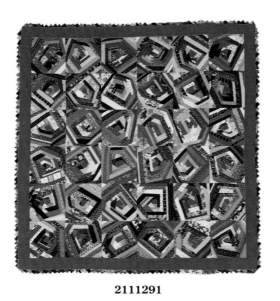

2111291

3111291

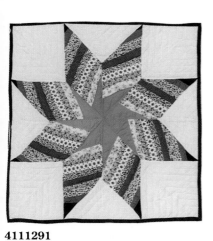

4111291

5111291

6111291

7111291

1111291 – RAINBOW BASKETS; 40" x 62"; shades of blue, violet, green & pink on black background; cotton & poly/cotton fabrics; polyester batting; made in Connecticut in 1990; machine pieced, quilted by hand in woven lattice design with grapevines in border. $218.00

2111291 – CRAZY QUILT; 108" x 108"; red center in each block with a red border, other prints, multi-colored; cotton; made in Colorado in 1991; machine pieced, hand quilted; light-weight polyester batting; unbleached muslin backing; more than 300 fabrics in design; prairie-point edging. $575.00

3111291 – DOUBLE IRISH CHAIN; 79" x 109"; blue & red; background red & white print; light blue printed lining; 100% cotton front & lining; made in Hawaii in 1991; machine pieced & quilted; 5 oz. bonded polyester batting. $322.00

4111291 – STAR; 32" x 32"; blue solids & prints, white background; machine pieced, hand quilted; polyester batting. $115.00

5111291 – TREE OF LIFE; 88" x 96"; blue, red, yellow, green leaves & binding; cotton & cotton blends; made in Indiana in 1989; all hand applique; polyester batting; County Fair winner. $1,035.00

6111291 – RED, HOT & BLUE, STARS & STEPPING STONES; 57" x 72"; red, white & blue with Orchid accent, white has small blue print on it; 100% cotton; made in Iowa in 1991; machine pieced, hand quilted; low loft polyester batting; finished with prairie points. $201.00

7111291 – TWINKLE, TWINKLE LITTLE STAR; 75" x 99"; blue background, green, pink, rust, navy & tan stars; cotton & cotton/poly fabrics; machine quilted & tied; polyester batting. $230.00

1121291

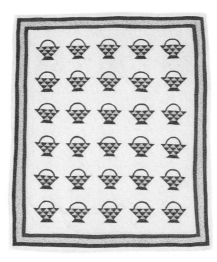

2121291

3121291

4121291

5121291

6121291

1121291 – VIRGINIA REEL (from a Judy Florence design); 39" x 56"; blue, purple, teal color range; cotton blends; made in 1991 in Minnesota; hand pieced & quilted; polyester batting; a variety of plaids & stripes. $207.00

2121291 – CHERRY BASKET; 78" x 88"; royal blue with light blue on white background; machine pieced, hand quilted; made in Illinois in 1991; polyester batting; quilted basket design in block. $276.00

3121291 – SUNBONNET SUE; 47" x 56"; pink, white & multicolored fabrics; cotton/poly blends; made in Idaho in 1991; hand quilted hearts, pink is tied; Mountain Mist batting. $70.00

4121291 – ROCK-A-BYE BABY; 35" x 45"; background mint green, horse purple & peach; 100% cottons; made in New York in 1991; machine pieced, hand quilted; polyester batting. $109.00

5121291 – MEDALLION PHEASANTS; 76" x 86"; navy blue & burgundy; 50/50 cotton/poly fabric; made in California in 1988; machine pieced & quilted; polyfil batting. $172.00

6121291 – TWENTY-FIVE PATCH; 53" x 70"; grays, blues, browns, reds, wines, tans & creams; cotton prints & plaids of the 1920's & 1930's; top probably made in 1920's, type of backing suggests it was finished in the 1940's or 1950's-shirting fabrics; hand pieced, hand quilted; quilt wasn't used much, if at all; two minor trunk stains. $199.00

7121291 – BEARS; 44" x 54"; solid yellow top & ruffle, green, pink, yellow balloons, back has white background; cotton/poly blend fabric; made in Pennsylvania in 1991; hand quilted; Dacron/poly batting. $86.00

7121291

14

1131291

2131291

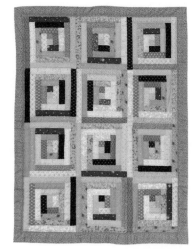

3131291

4131291

5131291

6131291

1131291 – PINEAPPLE; 26" x 26"; burgundy, pink, Hoffman wood block print; 100% cotton; made on Michigan's Keweenaw Peninsula late 1990; machine pieced, hand quilted (22 st/in counting both sides); each piece quilted with cable border; sleeve for hanging. $288.00

2131291 – HIDDEN WELLS II; 45" x 45"; blues & reds, florals, small prints, large prints & solids – a wide range of color values from light to dark; 100% cotton; made in Tennessee in 1990; machine pieced, hand quilted (there is a small amount of machine quilting, too – but invisible); curved quilting lines in border. $288.00

3131291 – LOG CABIN; 39" x 51"; light & dark blues; cotton & cotton blend fabrics; made in 1989 in Texas; machine pieced, hand quilted; polyester batting. $92.00

4131291 – CHECKERBOARD NINE PATCH; 36" x 36"; scrap quilt – mainly in blues; cotton fabrics (just a few cotton blends); made in California in 1991; machine pieced, hand quilted; Cotton Classic batting. $144.00

5131291 – SAIL BOATS; 31" x 46"; Williamsburg blue & white; 100% prewashed cotton, machine pieced, hand quilted; made in California in 1991; traditional batting. $144.00

6131291 – DANCE IN THE FOREST; 33" x 33"; mauve highlighted with dark rose, background off-white printed muslin; 100% cotton; made in Michigan in 1991; hand appliqued, quilted & hand-stuffed trapunto; mauve quilting thread; dark rose yarn used in trapunto. $367.00

7131291 – SUNSHINE & SHADOW; 39" x 44"; pastels/pinks, greens & blues; machine pieced, hand quilted; made in Georgia in 1990; polyester batting; sleeve on back for hanging. $88.00

15

1141291

2141291

3141291

4141291

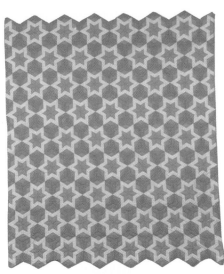

5141291

6141291

1141291 – WINTER COLORS; 30" x 33"; browns, beiges & off-whites; cottons & hand-painted cottons; made in Colorado in 1991; machine pieced & quilted, hand appliqued satin cording next to binding; Mountain Mist batting. $224.00

2141291 – ODD FELLOWS PATCH; 80" x 88"; navy blue & white; inside blue border & tiny quilting stitches done in ¾" grids; cotton fabrics; hand quilted; unknown maker 1875-1900; some repair work done on several small tears on the white background. $518.00

3141291 – MORE CUBIC TURTLES; 51" x 54"; turquoise & purple prints, solid turquoise backing; all 100% cotton Jenny Beyer Fabrics; made in Illinois in 1991; machine pieced, hand quilted; permanent rod pocket on back for hanging; diagonal quilting. $345.00

4141291 – FIRST LIGHT; 49" x 54"; background colors range from light blue to black; all fabrics are multicolored solids; cotton & cotton blends; made in Colorado in 1991; machine pieced, hand quilted; floral backing, low-loft batting. $299.00

5141291 – STARS & BLOCKS; 82" x 92"; plain blue with blue prints; cotton; made in Illinois in 1989; machine pieced, hand quilted; polyester batting. $345.00

6141291 – ENCIRCLED TULIP; 88" x 102"; shades of navy blue, rose & cream; all cotton; made in Kansas in 1991; machine pieced, hand quilted & appliqued; polyester batting, double binding, mitered corners. $477.00

7141291 – FLAG; 30" x 42"; red, white & blue; 100% cotton; made in Nebraska in 1991; hand quilted, machine pieced; polyfil polyester batting, hanging sleeve on back. $86.00

7141291

2151291

3151291

1151291

4151291

5151291

6151291

7151291

1151291 – UNKNOWN; 114" x 114"; white; cotton & polyester fabrics; made in Tennessee; hand quilted; small hearts & leaves in a circle, lace around each square; photo is darker & doesn't show detail. $431.00

2151291 – NINE PATCH; 39" x 39"; primary colors with white muslin background; 100% cottons; made in Georgia in 1990; machine pieced & hand quilted; solids & prints make up the nine patch blocks; polyester batting; black binding; quilted with white thread. $115.00

3151291 – PYRAMID; 80" x 90"; calico print blue, broadcloth trim, home-dyed muslin sheet lining; made in Tennessee in 1991; hand pieced & quilted; polyester batting. $230.00

4151291 – WEDGWOOD TULIP; 82" x 82"; Wedgwood blues on bleached muslin; made in New Jersey in 1988-89; hand quilted; polyester batting. $460.00

5151291 – SUNBURST or SUNFLOWER; 50" x 82"; multicolor with orange centers, teal; made in West Virginia area, quilted in 1989; machine pieced & quilted; white & burgundy sashes. $104.00

6151291 – BROKEN STAR; 96" x 97"; star in greens & peaches, background bleached muslin, backing muslin permapress; cottons & blends; machine pieced, hand quilted; made in Michigan in 1990; extraloft batting. $592.00

7151291 – WHEEL OF MYSTERY; 65" x 86"; mauve, black, gray & pink with a small off-white print background; 100% cotton; made in Florida in 1987-88; hand pieced & quilted; light batting; state fair red ribbon winner. $518.00

17

1161291

2161291

3161291

4161291

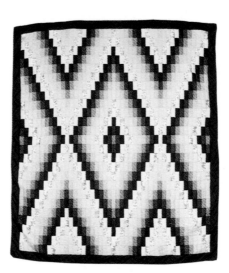

5161291

6161291

1161291 – LOG CABIN BARN RAISING; 78" x 105"; mauve center, light blue to dark blue, white background; cotton; made in Illinois in 1991; machine pieced, hand quilted; Dacron batting. $391.00

2161291 – QUEEN ANNE STAR; 90" x 108"; off-white; wholecloth fabric; made in West Virginia in 1991; hand quilted; Mountain Mist batting, material consists of resin treated polyester fiber, double stencil wholecloth quilt top, this is a close-up photo only. $489.00

3161291 – RED CENTER DIAMOND; 39" x 39"; black, red, purple & blue; broadcloth fabric, made in Pennsylvania in 1991; quilted with Amish stencils in an old traditional pattern with traditional colors, polyester batting, black backing. $230.00

4161291 – TRADITIONAL HEARTS CRIB QUILT; 36" x 42"; lavendar, off-white; 100% cotton broadcloth top with white cotton flannel back; made in California in 1991; machine pieced, hand appliqued & quilted; polyester fiberfill batting, quilting around each heart, border is a traditional woven chain. $138.00

5161291 – NAVAHO; 95" x 105"; shades of blue with some green, rose, cream in prints; polyester/cotton blends; made in Ohio in 1991; machine pieced, hand quilted; polyester batting. $518.00

6161291 – ROAD TO ST. LOUIS; 78" x 100"; rust & blue; cotton & cotton/polyester blend fabric; made in New Mexico 1990; machine pieced & quilted; polyester batting. $316.00

7161291 – DOUBLE IRISH CHAIN; 87" x 105"; country blue, brick red with light blue background; cotton & cotton/polyester blend fabrics; made in North Carolina in 1988; machine pieced with hand appliqued hearts, polyester batting, lots of hand quilting. $690.00

7161291

1171291

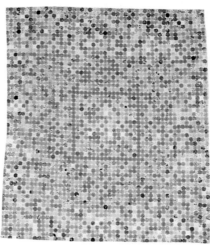

2171291

3171291

4171291

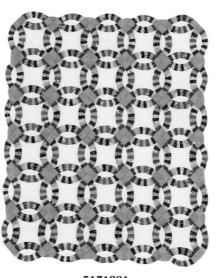

5171291

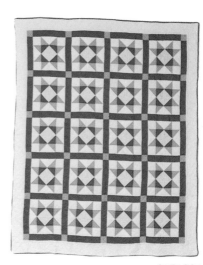

6171291

7171291

1171291 – VARIABLE STAR; 81" x 100"; cobalt blue & white; cotton; made in Pennsylvania in 1989; machine pieced, hand quilted. $431.00

2171291 – YO YO; 98" x 107"; multicolored prints; cotton & nylon; made in Indiana in 1980; completely handmade; no batting, quilt made of gathered circles. $575.00

3171291 – SAMPLER WALLHANGING; 40" x 40"; rose, sage green, colonial blue, black trim; cotton/poly blend; made in Kentucky in 1990; hand pieced & quilted; the center block flower only pressed on with Wonder-under®. $78.00

4171291 – A CHRISTIAN SOLDIER; 36" x 42"; yellow print frame, white background, center with figure hand painted in blue & gold fabric paint; cotton; made in Texas in 1991; machine pieced top, hand quilted; polyester batting, muslin lining, quilting includes outlining of figure & Christian symbols in each corner of quilt. $86.00

5171291 – DOUBLE WEDDING RING; 78" x 90"; bright multicolor prints, white background, one-piece white lining; cotton & cotton/polyester blends; made in Virginia in 1991; machine pieced, hand quilted, Polyfil Traditional batting, double bias binding. $345.00

6171291 – EVENING STAR; 90" x 108"; rose, pink & off-white; backing is tiny off-white print with rose; 100% cotton; made in Illinois in 1991; machine pieced, hand quilted; polyester batting, sashes are quilted in tulips, border is quilted in leaves. $443.00

7171291 – BEAR'S PAW; 87" x 104"; bold traditional Amish colors on black background; 100% cotton; made in Illinois in 1990; machine pieced, hand quilted in Amish designs. $632.00

19

1181291

2181291

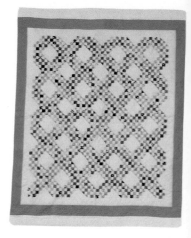

3181291

4181291

5181291

6181291

1181291 – LOVE RING VARIATION; 83" x 100"; blue; cotton/polyester fabrics; made in Missouri in 1991; machine pieced & quilted; polyester batting. $230.00

2181291 – LOG CABIN; 95" x 107"; pink & blue, pink backing; cotton & cotton/poly blends; made in California in 1988; hand quilted; polyester batting. $862.00

3181291 – IRISH CHAIN VARIATION; 82" x 100"; multicolor squares on white background with light blue border; all cotton; top was made in the 1970's, quilted in 1980 in Iowa; 50-50 poly/cotton fabrics. $316.00

4181291 – LONE STAR; 96" x 108"; dusty rose & dusty blue on off-white background; 100% cotton & cotton/poly blends; made by Mennonite women in Missouri in 1991; machine pieced, hand quilted; polyester batting. $402.00

5181291 – WHITE ON PERIWINKLE; 42" x 53"; off-white & periwinkle; 100% cottons; polyester batting; hand quilted (lots of hand quilting); the back is pictured since the blue backing will show the quilting better. $201.00

6181291 – MOUNTAIN MIST COLLAGE; 77" x 91"; green, light blue & navy background with multi-color appliqued; cotton fabric; made in Montana in 1987; hand appliqued, machine quilted; Mountain Mist Cotton Classic batting, 25 different traditional Mountain Mist patterns arranged into a pictorial quilt, sleeve for hanging. $402.00

7181291 – ANTIQUE CAR QUILT; 73" x 88"; red, navy, off-white background with sleeve on back for hanging; all cotton; made in Michigan in 1990; antique cars hand painted (colorfast paints), hand quilted, machine pieced; polyester batting, mitered corners. $675.00

7181291

1191291

2191291

3191291

4191291

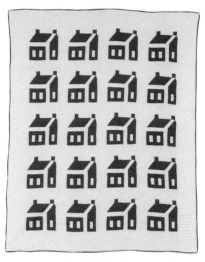

5191291

6191291

7191291

1191291 – LARGE 8 POINT BLOCK STAR; 88" x 108"; multicolor stars on white background with blue print border; 50/50 cotton/poly blend; made in central Missouri in 1989; machine pieced, hand quilted, Mountain Mist batting. $316.00

2191291 – NAUPAKA; 36" x 36"; shadow blue applique & border, white background, calico quilt backing; Imperial Broadcloth 40/60 cotton/polyester; hand appliqued & quilted; made in Marshall Islands in 1991; based on design by EA of Hawaii; quilted Hawaiian style with rows of quilting ½" apart. $288.00

3191291 – 'X' MARKS THE SPOT; 90" x 97"; yellow, red, black & blue; cotton fabrics; top made in Nebraska in the 1930's, outer backing & border are new; machine pieced, hand quilted. $259.00

4191291 – AMISH VIRGINIA STARS; 86" x 104"; Amish colors on traditional black background; 100% cotton; made in Illinois in 1991; machine pieced, hand quilted; emphasis on hand quilting. $690.00

5191291 – SCHOOLHOUSE; 78" x 94"; blue & white; cotton; made in Texas in 1991; hand pieced & quilted; Mountain Mist batting. $345.00

6191291 – UNKNOWN; 84" x 101"; olive green stems/leaves with burgundy roses & binding, white background; cotton/polyester fabric; probably made about seven years ago; machine appliqued, hand quilted. $460.00

7191291 – TULIP PATCHWORK; 87" x 101"; multicolor with sky blue & white; cotton/polyester fabrics; made in Illinois in 1989; machine pieced, hand quilted. $374.00

1010392

2010392

3010392

4010392

5010392

6010392

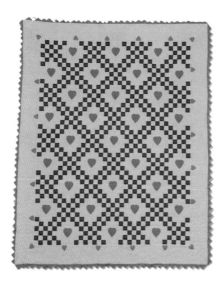

7010392

1010392 – LOG CABIN - BARN RAISING; 82" x 106; shades of blue prints, the lining matches one of the prints used in the quilt; cotton; made in New York in 1989; machine pieced, hand quilted; mitered corners, double binding, Dacron™ polyester batting, all fabrics prewashed. $460.00

2010392 – CITY TRAFFIC; 28" x 35"; navy chintz w/scraps of more than 40 fabrics; all cotton; made in Pennsylvania in 1986; machine pieced, hand quilted; Mountain Mist Quilt Light batting; wall or doll quilt w/sleeve for hanging, quilt stencil design on border. $115.00

3010392 – TUMBLING STAR; 84" x 100"; burgundy stars, off-white blocks, wine print, white lining; cotton; made in Alabama in 1989; machine pieced, hand quilted on each side of seam; polyester batting; color coordinated using burgundy as dominant color, burgundy quilt binding. $402.00

4010392 – RAILROAD FENCE; 77" x 91"; navy, rust, cream & blue; 100% cotton; made in Illinois in 1988; machine pieced, hand quilted; quilted in the ditch, delicate light blue color, chintz material. $264.00

5010392 – FLORAL BOUQUET; 76" x 104; pink & maroon on white w/green accents; 100% cotton; made in Illinois in 1990; hand appliqued & quilted; Mountain Mist batting. $345.00

6010392 – FLOWER BUDS; 86" x 105"; soft gray-blue w/pale yellow flowers on off-white background; 100% cotton prints, prewashed; made in Wisconsin in 1990; machine pieced & quilted; polyester batting; pleasing soft colors & simple pattern. $230.00

7010392 – DOUBLE IRISH CHAIN; 86" x 102"; country blue & dusty rose w/white background, the border is dusty rose prairie points; all cotton; made in 1991 in Kansas; machine pieced, hand quilted & appliqued hearts; Hobbs polyester batting; quilted with little scallops around each heart & border. $448.00

22

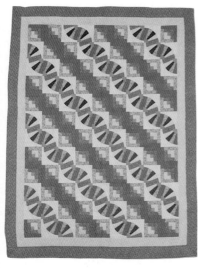

1020392

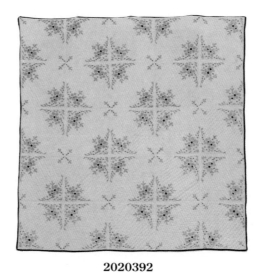

2020392

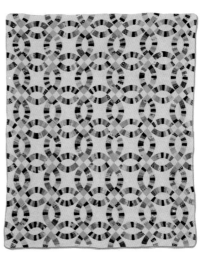

3020392

4020392

5020392

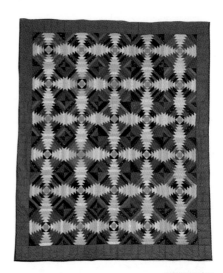

6020392

1020392 – LOG CABIN FAN; 80" x 102"; shades of rose, pink & cream w/white; all cotton; made in Kansas in 1991; machine pieced, hand quilted; polyester batting, mitered corners, double binding. $414.00

2020392 – CROSS STITCH FLOWER; 84" x 84"; white background w/peachy orange flowers, brown; cotton & cotton/polyester blends; made in Arkansas in 1989; hand pieced, quilted & embroidered; polyester batting, double bias binding. $230.00

3020392 – WEDDING RING; 80" x 92"; blue squares joining w/blue binding, bright colors in prints & solids; cotton; made in the 1930's in Missouri; all hand made; thin batting, tiny hand stitching, much quilting in area between rings & surrounding areas. $402.00

4020392 – COLONIAL GIRL; 78" x 97"; brown calico, off-white; cotton/polyester; made in Illinois in 1991; machine pieced, quilted & appliqued, machine quilted in cloud design. $288.00

5020392 – RAIL FENCE; 92" x 110"; red, yellow & blue; cotton/polyester; made in Illinois in 1990; machine pieced, hand quilted; reversible quilt. $144.00

6020392 – PINEAPPLE; 83" x 98"; light & dark blue; cotton/polyester; made in Missouri in 1991; machine pieced, hand quilted; polyester batting. $402.00

7020392 – LOG CABIN – BARN RAISING; 88" x 108"; browns, golds including tans, greens, bronze & orange, natural color muslin backing; cotton & cotton blend fabrics, cotton muslin backing; made in Minnesota in 1991; tied quilt; both old & new fabrics, new condition. $167.00

7020392

1030392

2030392

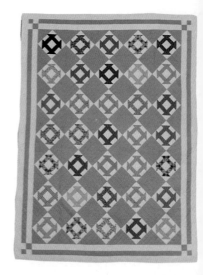

3030392

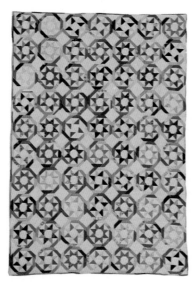

4030392

5030392

6030392

7030392

1030392 – IRISH CHAIN; 81" x 98"; dusty blue on white background; cotton & cotton/polyester blend fabrics; made in Wisconsin in 1991; machine pieced, hand quilted; polyester batting. $270.00

2030392 – AN AUGUST GARDEN; 80" x 80"; soft yellow, mauve, lavender, cream, sage green & caramel; cotton; made in California in 1991; machine pieced & quilted; Cotton Classic batting; blocks are set on point and are abstract representations of flowers. $288.00

3030392 – MONKEY WRENCH; 77" x 102"; lavender on white w/multicolored fabrics, soft green checkerboard back; made in Illinois in 1989; machine pieced, hand quilted; traditional pattern gives Depression-era look; Mountain Mist batting. $264.00

4030392 – JUDY'S STAR; 73" x 104"; blues, green, pink & various prints; mostly cotton w/some polyester/cotton, background & backing washed muslin; made in Arkansas in 1991; machine pieced, hand quilted on both sides of seam, double bias binding. $259.00

5030392 – RAIL FENCE; 93" x 106"; brown back, large yellow brown flower prints, small brown flower prints; cotton/polyester blends; made in Illinois in 1990; machine pieced, hand quilted; Dacron™ polyester Super Fluff batting. $144.00

6030392 – LOG CABIN; 86" x 107"; blue; cotton; made in Texas in 1991; machine pieced, hand quilted; prewashed materials, Mountain Mist batting. $345.00

7030392 – MANY TRIPS AROUND THE WORLD; 92" x 106"; rose w/blue & cream; polyester/cotton blend fabrics; made in Ohio in 1991; machine pieced, hand quilted; polyester batting. $460.00

1040392

2040392

3040392

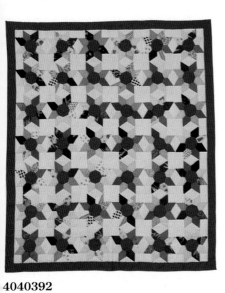

4040392

5040392

6040392

1040392 – WINDOW PANE; 52" x 63"; black floral quilt w/tan, green & red accents; 100% cotton; made in Iowa in 1991; machine pieced & quilted; backing has unique pieced center panel; Fairfield Traditional 100% polyester batting; hand finished binding. $172.00

2040392 – COLOR CHAIN STAR; 92" x 99"; blue; cotton/polyester; made in Missouri in 1991; machine pieced, hand quilted; polyester batting. $402.00

3040392 – SINGLE IRISH CHAIN; 88" x 100"; berry, green & paisley; 100% cotton; made in Alabama in 1991; machine pieced, hand quilted; bonded polyester batting; quilted in 1" grid on 16" drop, main pattern floating in center of quilt. $690.00

4040392 – FRIENDSHIP STAR; 80" x 92"; multicolored prints & solids; cotton & cotton/-polyester blends; made in Arkansas in 1990; hand & machine pieced, hand quilted; polyester batting; solid blue broadcloth centers, set together w/muslin, quilted in border & around each seam. $230.00

5040392 – FRIENDSHIP BASKET; 93" x 102"; multicolored; cotton/polyester; made in Missouri in 1991; hand & machine pieced, hand quilted; polyester batting. $402.00

6040392 – TRIP AROUND THE WORLD; 40" x 53"; blue, peach, purple, yellow, rose & green; 100% cottons, made in Colorado in 1991; machine pieced, hand quilted; polyester batting. $144.00

7040392 – TRIP AROUND THE WORLD; 81" x 95"; peach & brown; 100% cotton; made in Iowa in 1991; machine pieced, hand quilted, quilted in the ditch, rope border design; polyester batting; one piece cream back w/small white roses, double fold bias binding. $460.00

7040392

1050392

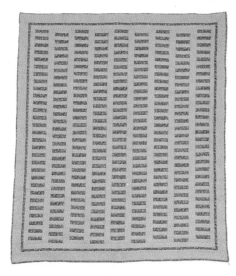

2050392

3050392

4050392

5050392

6050392

7050392

1050392 – IRIS; 88" x 96"; white background, purple, orchid, red, pink, red, yellow, green leaves & stems, green binding; permapress & cotton blends; made in Indiana in 1991; all hand made & appliqued, polyester batting. $1,035.00

2050392 – STEVEN'S QUILT; 89" x 102"; blue & coral; cotton; made in New York in 1990; machine pieced, hand quilted; prewashed fabrics; polyester batting, reversible. $575.00

3050392 – PRAIRIE PINES; 56" x 68"; tan, cream, turkey reds, greens, browns w/tan backing; cotton; made in Nebraska in 1991; machine pieced, hand quilted; polyester batting. $230.00

4050392 – ORIGINAL DESIGN BASED ON CARPENTER'S WHEEL; 84" x 92"; pinks, off white, pink/green print; cotton top, cotton/polyester backing; made in New York in 1991; machine pieced & quilted; extra-loft polyester batting; quilted in a heart design. $431.00

5050392 – LOG CABIN – BARN RAISING; 83" x 102"; light blue & white; cotton & cotton blend fabrics; made in Indiana in 1991; machine pieced & quilted; polyester batting; backing is bleached muslin; the extra length of quilt to cover pillows makes shams unnecessary. $201.00

6050392 – AMERICAN REVOLUTION; 64" x 91"; red, white & blue w/small amounts of green, brown & rust; cotton & cotton/poly blends; made in Minnesota in 1991; hand quilted, embroidered & appliqued; poly-fil batting. $460.00

7050392 – DRESDEN PLATE; 85" x 102"; blue & rose, multicolored plate, white background; all cotton with cotton/poly backing; made in Kansas in 1991; machine pieced, hand appliqued & quilted; 100% polyester batting; quilted heart & roses; mitered corners & double bias binding. $437.00

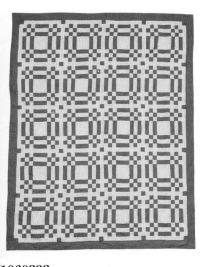

1060392

2060392

3060392

4060392

5060392

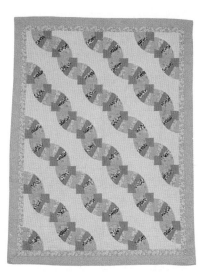

6060392

1060392 – NINE PATCH VARIATION; 88" x 106"; blue with white background; cotton/polyester; made in Missouri in 1991; machine pieced & quilted; polyester batting. $230.00

2060392 – DUCK PANELS; 82" x 86"; duck panels w/sold tan blocks, bright rust geese border; cotton & cotton blends; made in Idaho in 1991; machine pieced, hand quilted; polyester batting, cotton backing; duck panels have teflon sheen, solid blocks quilted w/complementing cattail design; border of Flying Geese. $454.00

3060392 – LOG CABIN; 82" x 110"; blue & pink; 100% cotton top, back is cotton/polyester blend; made in Wisconsin in 1991; machine pieced & quilted, quilted w/hearts & tulips motif; Fairfield medium thick polyester batting. $259.00

4060392 – SCRAP BASKETS; 70" x 84"; peaches & blues; 100% cotton; made in Wisconsin in 1991; machine pieced & quilted; extra loft polyester batting. $345.00

5060392 – LOG CABIN WITH STAR CENTER; 98" x 108"; off-white background, seafoam green & brown calicos w/plain tan; broadcloth fabric; made in Pennsylvania in 1991; machine pieced, hand quilted; polyester batting. $460.00

6060392 – GRANDMOTHER'S FAN; 85" x 106"; shades of pink on cream background; all cotton; made in Kansas in 1991; machine pieced, hand quilted; each block is trimmed in poly lace & quilted in tiny squares & little bows; double binding, mitered corners; polyester batting. $431.00

7060392 – SQUARE IN A SQUARE; 86" x 101"; black & white; cotton/polyester; made in Missouri in 1991; machine pieced & quilted; polyester batting. $230.00

7060392

1070392

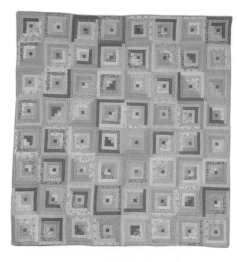

2070392

3070392

4070392

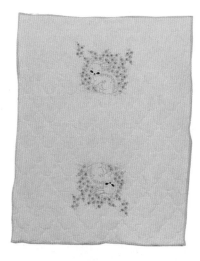

5070392

6070392

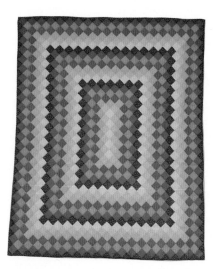

7070392

1070392 – PANDA BEARS; 45" x 62"; mint green backing, white background, pastel rainbow & balloon on front; poly/cotton fabrics; made in Pennsylvania in 1991; hand quilted; Dacron™ polyester batting. $86.00

2070392 – LOG CABIN; 98" x 104"; a soft blend of baby blues & delicate peach shades; 100% cotton; made in Tennessee in 1990; machine pieced, hand quilted. $632.00

3070392 – UNKNOWN; 72" x 82"; variegated prints, green binding, white lining; cotton & cotton blends; made in 1989 in West Virginia; polyester batting. $172.00

4070392 – MARINER'S COMPASS; 80" x 101"; shades of blue & rose, background print includes leaves of darkest green; 100% prewashed cotton, seamless muslin backing; made in Wisconsin in 1991; hand & machine pieced, quilted using "heirloom machine quilting" (quilt appears handmade); polyester batting. $328.00

5070392 – BUNNIES IN THE GARDEN; 42" x 53"; white front w/embroidery, blue back; cotton; made in South Dakota in 1991; machine quilted; polyester batting; matching pillow included. $75.00

6070392 – PHEASANT; 55" x 46"; background is buckskin, leaves are light brown & light green; bird is browns & turquoises; 100% cotton, velveteen & ultrasuede; made in New York in 1991; machine pieced, hand appliqued & quilted; poly fill batting; prewashed; leaves hand dyed; hand quilted leaves & cattails in background. $288.00

7070392 – TRIP AROUND THE WORLD; 86" x 100"; blue & rose; cottons; made in Pennsylvania in 1991; machine pieced & quilted; bonded polyester batting, double binding, light blue back. $374.00

1080392

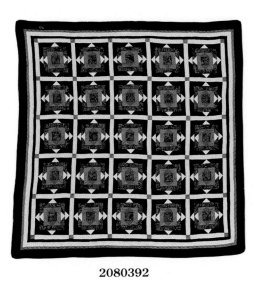

2080392

3080392

4080392

5080392

6080392

1080392 – LOVE WITHOUT MONEY; 39" x 39"; pink, black, white, blue-green, green, yellow; cotton fabrics; made in Massachusetts in 1987; machine pieced, hand quilted, strip pieced; cotton batting & back; some vintage fabrics from Grandmother's scrap bag included, ready to hang. $310.00

2080392 – PAISLEY SQUARE; 80" x 80"; lavender, paisley, black, white & rose; cotton; made in Wisconsin in 1990; hand pieced & quilted; Mountain Mist polyester batting. $345.00

3080392 – FLOWER GARDEN; 80" x 95"; all pastel shades on white, yellow centers; cotton fabrics; made in Illinois in 1991; machine pieced, hand quilted; polyester batting, new materials. $288.00

4080392 – SHEEP IN CLOVER; 72" x 92"; spring green & white; cotton fabrics; made in Illinois in 1991; machine pieced, hand quilted & appliqued; polyester batting; a shepherdess is watching her sheep in a pasture of clover aided by 12 little girls. $345.00

5080392 – DAHLIA; 96" x 110"; dusty blue, peach, off-white background; cotton/polyester & cotton fabrics; made in Missouri in 1991; machine pieced, hand quilted; Mennonite-made; Dacron™ batting. $437.00

6080392 – TENNESSEE WALTZ; 71" x 89"; pink & black w/beige, large floral backing; all cottons; made in California in 1991; machine pieced, hand quilted; polyester batting. $402.00

7080392 – CELTIC APPLIQUE SAMPLER; 86" x 102"; colonial blues on off-white background; cotton & cotton blends; made in Wisconsin in 1991; hand appliqued & quilted; Mountain Mist batting; washed once. $690.00

7080392

1090392

2090392

3090392

4090392

5090392

6090392

7090392

1090392 – FLORAL ARRAY; 84" x 105"; pastel rose & green, off-white; 100% cotton & a polished sheen fabric; made in Ohio in 1991; blind stitched, hand applique & quilting w/designs of florals, shells, hearts & vines; polyester batting. $546.00

2090392 – GRANDMOTHER'S FLOWER GARDEN; 88" x 100"; solid red, yellow print flowers w/blue path, blue & red border; cotton blends; made in Kentucky in 1990; hand pieced & quilted; polyester batting, quilted by the piece, quilting on the borders. $431.00

3090392 – LOVE RING; 96" x 103"; medium blue, green, peach, mauve; cotton/polyester; hand pieced & quilted; made in Missouri in 1991; polyester batting. $345.00

4090392 – BLOCK OF THE MONTH; 87" x 102"; blues & mauves on unbleached muslin; 100% cotton; made in Alabama in 1991; machine pieced, hand quilted; Hobbs poly down batting; blocks represent 12 months; model for teaching a "block of the month" quilting class. $920.00

5090392 – AMERICAN STARS IN THE SAND; 92" x 109"; light & dark teal green, teal green & lavender print on sand background, white backing; cotton; made in Michigan in 1991; machine pieced, hand quilted; polyester batting; made to commemorate the Persian Gulf War; has rod pocket, double binding. $574.00

6090392 – HAWAIIAN; 82" x 82"; green applique w/off-white background; cotton; construction of quilt began in the 1940's in Hawaii & finished in Alabama in 1991; hand quilted & appliqued; poly down batt; original Hawaiian design, hand quilted in echo design. $1,035.00

7090392 – STAR & HEARTS; 88" x 102"; shades of navy & mauve; cotton w/polyester batting; made in Kansas in 1991; machine pieced, hand quilted & appliqued; double binding, mitered corners. $431.00

1100392

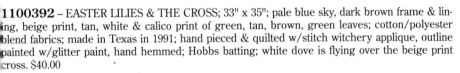

2100392

3100392

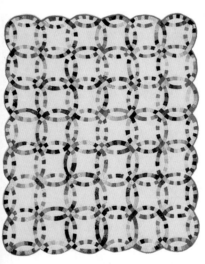

4100392

5100392

6100392

1100392 – EASTER LILIES & THE CROSS; 33" x 35"; pale blue sky, dark brown frame & lining, beige print, tan, white & calico print of green, tan, brown, green leaves; cotton/polyester blend fabrics; made in Texas in 1991; hand pieced & quilted w/stitch witchery applique, outline painted w/glitter paint, hand hemmed; Hobbs batting; white dove is flying over the beige print cross. $40.00

2100392 – FLOWER GARDEN; 100" x 100"; different prints w/off-white lining; polyester & cotton fabrics; made in Tennessee in 1986; machine pieced, hand quilted; polyester batting. $575.00

3100392 – OLD FASHIONED ROSE; 77" x 107"; red, green & white; prewashed all cotton materials; made in Kentucky in 1991; hand quilted & appliqued; Mountain Mist batting. $460.00

4100392 – DOUBLE WEDDING RING; 84" x 97"; multicolored w/white background; cotton/polyester; made in Missouri in 1991; machine pieced, hand quilted; polyester batting. $345.00

5100392 – BOATS AHOY; 44" x 45"; navy blue base w/red border, multicolored boats w/white sails; 100% cotton; made in New Jersey in 1991; machine pieced, hand quilted; prewashed fabrics, Fairfield 100% Polyester Traditional Batting; this design is a variation of a pattern called "Sails in the Sunset" from a Georgia Bonsteel Lap Quilting book. $230.00

6100392 – SAMPLER; 85" x 100"; blues, reds, yellow & browns on ecru background; cotton & cotton blends; made in 1985 in Indiana; hand pieced & quilted; Mountain Mist batting; received a special merit award in county fair. $575.00

7100392 – MORNING STARS; 85" x 101"; rose, country blue, cream background (w/tiny country blue heart patterned fabric); 100% prewashed cotton; made in Illinois in 1991; hand quilted, machine pieced; Mountain Mist batting; intricately quilted. $460.00

7100392

31

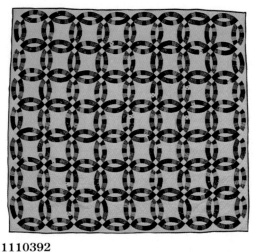

1110392

2110392

3110392

4110392

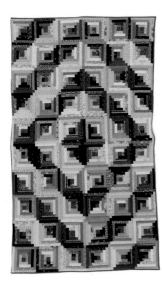

5110392

6110392

7110392

1110392 – WEDDING RING; 96" x 108"; peach & browns; made in Delaware in 1991; machine pieced, hand quilted; new quilt. $908.00

2110392 – CHURN DASH; 72" x 99"; blue w/white background; cotton/polyester; made in Missouri in 1991; machine pieced & quilted; polyester batting. $172.00

3110392 – DOUBLE WEDDING RING; 87" x 101"; blue, mauve, off-white background muslin, cotton/polyester blends; made in Missouri in 1991; machine pieced, hand quilted bonded poly batting; rings are blue & mauve; quilted seam by seam. $345.00

4110392 – CABIN PATH; 95" x 104; red, white & blue; cotton; made in Alabama in 1991 machine pieced, hand quilted on each side of seam; original pattern; polyester batting, sheet lining. $460.00

5110392 – LOG CABIN–BARN RAISING; 54" x 91"; multicolored w/red chimneys, bound in matching red; 100% cotton; made in Delaware in 1991; machine pieced, hand quilted; muslin backing, bias bound; scrap quilt with 60 squares, 1" logs, quilted down the center of each log. $345.00

6110392 – SIX POINT STAR; 71" x 91"; multicolored print stars w/solid centers, two shades of green border, muslin background & backing, prints are in blues, browns, reds & greens; cotton/polyester blends; made in Ohio in 1989; hand pieced & quilted; polyester batting. $489.00

7110392 – GRANDMOTHER'S FLOWER GARDEN; 74" x 81"; pastels bordered by white, bordered by pastels; 100% cotton; made in Georgia in 1990; machine pieced, hand quilted; polyester batting; pastel prints & solids make up "flower," paths are white, bordered by turquoise strip & yellow plaid strip, backing is white 100% cotton sheeting without seams, binding is light turquoise bias tape, lots of quilting. $460.00

1120392

2120392

3120392

4120392

5120392

6120392

1120392 – GIANT DAHLIA; 80" x 98"; rose, blue, rose & blue print, pink w/some burgundy, off-white background; cotton/polyester, 100% cotton muslin backing; made in Wisconsin in 1989; fiber-fil one sheet batting. $447.00

2120392 – BANBURY CROSS; 78" x 98"; blue, brown, peach & rust; cottons; made in Michigan in 1989; machine pieced, hand quilted; Polyfil Ultraloft batting, muslin back, double binding. $552.00

3120392 – FEATHERED STAR & FLOWERS; 45" x 45"; black, pink & green floral print w/pink & green applique, white-on-white background; 100% cotton; made in Louisiana in 1991; machine pieced, hand appliqued & quilted; Fairfield polyester batting; matching pink backing, quilted in pink thread, double binding (hand sewn); original design by maker. $460.00

4120392 – OLD PATTERN QUILT; 63" x 63"; white, green & red; cotton/polyester blend; made in Idaho in 1991; hand quilted & appliqued; Mountain Mist batting; even though the pattern name is not known by the maker, the pattern was taken from an old quilt made in 1898. $126.00

5120392 – SCRAPAHOLIC IN BARNRAISING SETTING; 35" x 46"; forest green borders w/multiple colors in scrap pieces; cottons; made in Florida in 1988; machine pieced, hand quilted in neutral thread on light piecing areas & the border; Mountain Mist light batting; green floral print backing & hanging sleeve, ¼" binding has mitered corners. $115.00

6120392 – SWIMMERS IN THE SEA; 31" x 31"; teals, lavenders, navy print; 100% cotton, designer prints; made in Tennessee in 1991; machine pieced & quilted, embellished w/metallic thread; pictorial wall quilt of fish swimming in the reef. $213.00

7120392 – PRIMROSE WREATH; 82" x 100"; blue & green on beige; cotton & cotton blends; made in Ohio in 1990; hand quilted & appliqued. $690.00

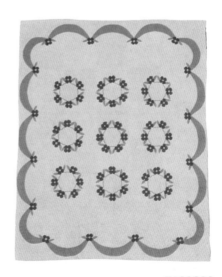

7120392

1130392

2130392

3130392

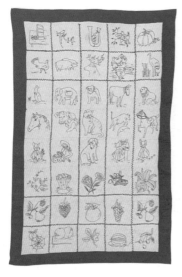

4130392

5130392

6130392

7130392

1130392 – KALEIDOSCOPE; 31" x 31"; purples, muslin backing; all cotton print fabrics; made in Washington in 1991; machine pieced, hand quilted; low-loft polyester batting, hanging sleeve. $144.00

2130392 – SKYSCOPE #3 – CLOUD TREADER; 59" x 90"; red, green, purple, black & white w/white reverse side; cotton & blends; made in Massachusetts in 1990; machine pieced, hand quilted; Mountain Mist batting; won a prize in an art exhibition. $345.00

3130392 – BLUE WREATH / LOG CABIN; 38" x 38"; multicolored solids, bright blue border, light blue backing, black binding; 100% cotton, made in Virginia in 1991; machine pieced, hand quilted; low loft polyester batting, heavily quilted, hanging sleeve attached. $150.00

4130392 – EMBROIDERED CRIB QUILT; 42" x 64"; white background, red embroidery; cotton; made c.1940, maker unknown; machine pieced, hand quilted & embroidered; cotton batting. $325.00

5130392 – RABBITS, RABBITS, RABBITS; 33" x 41"; pastels of pinks, blues, lavenders & light red, background is white with ⅔" pink tulips overall; 100% cotton; made in Washington in 1990; machine pieced, hand quilted, some embroidery (whiskers, nose, etc.) & "3-D" rabbit ears. $70.00

6130392 – ANIMAL TREE; 40" x 50"; greens, browns & primary colors w/muslin background; 100% cotton; made in Arkansas in 1991; hand appliqued, embroidered & quilted; polyfil thin batting, outline quilting & small clamshell, embellished w/beaded eyes on "creatures," handmade bias binding. $144.00

7130392 – DRESDEN PLATE; 78" x 92" multicolored design w/ blue blocks & blue border; cotton; finished in Iowa in 1989; machine stitched the plate together, hand embroidered, appliqued & stitched; traditional Mountain Mist batting. $316.00

34

1140392

2140392

3140392

4140392

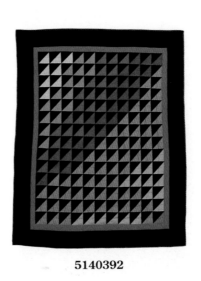

5140392

6140392

1140392 – 9 PATCH IN A 9 PATCH; 30" x 30"; red & blue prints, muslin; cotton; made in North Carolina in 1991; machine pieced & quilted; it has 477 pieces, Cotton Classic batting. $144.00

2140392 – DOUBLE WEDDING RING; 90" x 101"; dark blue top, off-white center pieces on top, off-white lining; percale; made in Tennessee in 1991; hand & machine pieced, hand quilted; Polyfil polyester batting. $402.00

3140392 – 8 POINT BLOCK STAR; 84" x 98"; rust & white w/tan print, predominantly white background; cotton & polyester; made in Iowa in 1989; machine sewn top, hand quilted; Mountain Mist batting. $316.00

4140392 – LITTLE CINNAMON BEARS; 73" x 86"; cinnamon, off-white, cinnamon & white tiny calico print; cotton & cotton/polyester; made in Arizona in 1991; machine pieced, hand quilted; Mountain Mist batting; bears quilted in framing & hearts quilted in edge (not seen in photo well), red backing & binding, double quilted. $460.00

5140392 – LEFTOVER TRIANGLES; 41" x 49"; bright solids on black triangles, bordered by bright turquoise strip & black 4" border, backing is navy/white plaid, purple binding; 100% pre-washed cotton fabrics; made in Georgia in 1991; machine pieced, hand quilted; Hobbs dark batting w/black thread; sleeve for hanging. $230.00

6140392 – HEXAGONS; 74" x 89"; multicolored scraps, yellow backing & binding; cotton; top made by machine c.1950, quilted more recently by hand; polyester batting; a few very tiny stains, otherwise excellent condition. $288.00

7140392 – SUNBONNET GIRL; 83" x 99"; multicolors on white w/pink borders; cotton & blends; made in Missouri in 1989; machine appliqued & quilted; polyester batting, white lining. $172.00

7140392

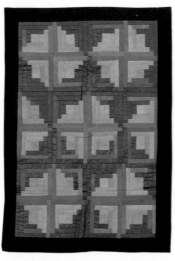

1150392

2150392

3150392

4150392

5150392

6150392

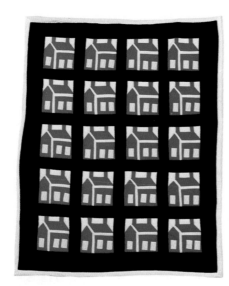

7150392

1150392 – LOG CABIN; 29" x 41"; brown background (some chintz), rose, apricot, light blue & green; 100% cotton; made in Georgia in 1990; machine pieced, hand tied; polyester batting; all fabrics except browns are hand-dyed w/Procion dyes; subtle hue variations. $141.00

2150392 – PINWHEEL 39" x 39"; mauve, blue & white-on-white print; back is white-on-white print; 100% cotton; made in Illinois in 1991; machine pieced, hand quilted; polyester batting; loops on back for hanging quilt. $121.00

3150392 – NAVY STARS; 84" x 92"; navy, cream & rust; 100% cotton; made in Nebraska in 1990; machine pieced, hand quilted; polyester batting. $345.00

4150392 – DRESDEN PLATE; 40" x 40"; blue & white tones; cotton/polyester; made in Illinois in 1990; hand appliqued & quilted. $109.00

5150392 – ROMAN SQUARES; 62" x 81"; predominantly red & navy w/yellow highlights; all prewashed cotton; made in South Carolina in 1990; machine pieced, hand quilted; polyester low-loft batting; extensive quilting in the ditch & through block squares; one border red denim print, the other border navy. $437.00

6150392 – FLOWER REEL VARIATION; 60" x 67"; white w/yellow, pink, green, blue prints, off-white border w/green & pink, light green calico print backing; 100% cotton top; made in California in 1990; machine & hand pieced, hand appliqued & quilted; traditional polyester batting; off-white border is appliqued w/seafoam green vine & leaves & pink calico tulips, pink double fold binding. $391.00

7150392 – LITTLE RED SCHOOL HOUSE; 70" x 86"; red, black & white; all cottons; made in Georgia in 1989; hand pieced & quilted; polyester batting; primitive. $230.00

1160392

2160392

3160392

4160392

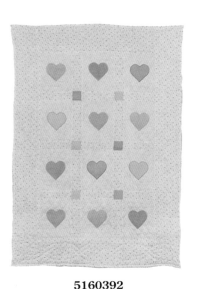

5160392

6160392

1160392 – SNOWBALL & NINE PATCH; 70" x 86"; white, blue & red; cotton & cotton/-polyester blends; made in Arkansas in 1989; machine pieced, hand quilted & tied w/blue yarn in the nine patch squares; poly fil batting; very pale blue w/tiny floral cotton/poly batting; binding matches medium blue print in quilt top. $230.00

2160392 – ROSE OF SHARON; 80" x 102"; rose, pink, pea green w/white background; cotton; made in New Mexico in 1991; hand pieced & appliqued, strips sewn on by machine; double quilted hearts all around border, quilted flowers in corners, set together w/rose strips. $575.00

3160392 – PENNSYLVANIA STAR; 92" x 98"; blue; cotton/polyester; made in Missouri in 1990; machine pieced, hand quilted; polyester batting. $402.00

4160392 – WHISPERING SANDS – NAVAJO PATTERN; 106" x 114"; permapress shell; made in California in 1991; machine pieced, hand quilted; Mountain Mist batting. $489.00

5160392 – HEARTS CRIB QUILT; 36" x 50"; multicolored tiny hearts print appliqued on white background; cotton/polyester blend; made in Illinois in 1991; machine appliqued, hand quilted. $86.00

6160392 – MOUNTAIN LAUREL; 94" x 94"; rose, cream, blue & green; cotton; made in Pennsylvania in 1990; machine pieced, hand quilted & appliqued; polyester batting; original c.1900 blocks incorporated into a unique design. $518.00

7160392 – BEAR PAW; 87" x 106"; blue, rust, red w/background cream w/blue print; all cotton prints; made in Michigan in 1991; machine pieced, hand quilted; Mountain Mist batting; pieced paw border is 3" wide; there are 48 – 10½" blocks, outside border is 6½" of dark blue, separate matching bias binding. $748.00

7160392

1170392

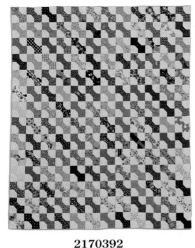

2170392

3170392

4170392

5170392

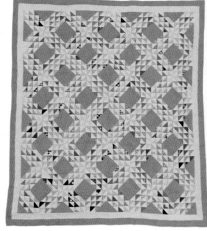

6170392

7170392

1170392 – FLOWER GARDEN BASKET; 80" x 86"; white w/rose, yellow & green; cotton & cotton blends; made in Arkansas in 1989; hand pieced & quilted; polyester batting; minor spot. $230.00

2170392 – BOWTIE; 76" x 89"; bowties made of multicolored prints, muslin background, light blue binding & backing; cotton/polyester fabrics; made in Kentucky in 1981; hand pieced & quilted; polyester batting; pillow included. $489.00

3170392 – EVENING STAR; 72" x 72"; navy w/small white star print, white background; cotton; made in New Mexico in 1903; blocks are hand pieced, blocks & border assembled by machine; cotton batting; two small stains, slight wear at one corner; embroidery on back reads "finished 1903 and quilted from 16 of March to 26 of May 1903 E.L.R." $1,006.00

4170392 – BALTIMORE BRIDE; 96" x 96"; multicolored w/white background; muslin; made in Indiana in 1991; hand cross stitched & embroidered from an old kit; polyester batting. $690.00

5170392 – CONTEMPORARY WINDOWS; 39" x 39"; different shades of green w/burgundy accents on white; 100% prewashed cotton; made in New York in 1991; machine pieced, hand quilted; contemporary windows with "in the ditch" quilting on point; low loft batting. $230.00

6170392 – OCEAN WAVES; 84" x 90"; rose print pattern blocks, all colors in triangles w/light yellow pinwheels; rose border; cotton; made in Kansas in 1930's; hand pieced & quilted; thin batting; recently washed; leaf & vine quilting in two borders. $489.00

7170392 – TULIP; 88" x 108"; old rose & rust w/green leaves on white; all cotton with cotton/poly blend backing; made in Kansas in 1989; machine pieced, hand appliqued & quilted; polyester batting; mitered corners & double binding. $518.00

1180392

2180392

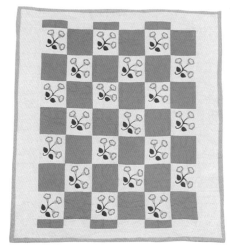

3180392

4180392

5180392

6180392

1180392 – GRANDMOTHER'S FAN; 82" x 98"; shades of mauve or rose w/green & blue in floral on cream; all cotton top w/polyester/cotton backing; made in Kansas in 1991; machine pieced, hand quilted; polyester batting; mitered corners, double binding. $448.00

2180392 – FLOWERS; 90" x 90"; red & green on white; all cotton; made in Pennsylvania; hand quilted; sawtooth border w/piping; signed & dated December 16, 1862; cotton batting. $2,530.00

3180392 – POPPIES; 89" x 95"; off-white, blue, light green border & backing, dark green stems & leaves; cottons; made in Maryland in 1990; hand appliqued & quilted; Mountain Mist batting; appliqued poppies alternating w/quilted poppies – the dark green stems & leaves are also appliqued. $494.00

4180392 – BOW TIE; 74" x 78"; various solids & prints; cotton & cotton blends; made in Kentucky in 1990; hand & machine pieced, machine quilted; polyester batting. $172.00

5180392 – SOUTH PORT LIGHTHOUSE; 50" x 51"; red, white, navy w/blue background; cotton & cotton/polyester; made in Wisconsin in 1990; hand & machine pieced & quilted, hand embroidered; polyester bonded batting. $86.00

6180392 – PONTIAC STAR; 100" x 110"; multicolored star w/white background & red border; cotton/polyester 50/50 blend; made in Missouri in 1989; top is machine sewn, the rest completely hand quilted; Mountain Mist batting. $345.00

7180392 – TURNING TRIANGLES; 78" x 90"; multicolored prints & solids, light blue border, white background; cottons & cotton/polyester blends; made in Arkansas in 1990; machine pieced, hand quilted; polyester batting; design quilted in border. $230.00

7180392

1190392

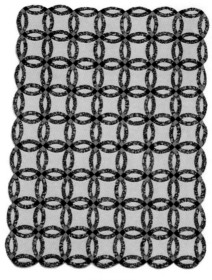

2190392

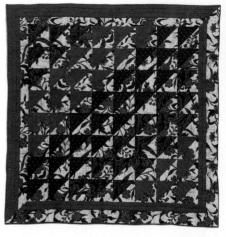

3190392

4190392

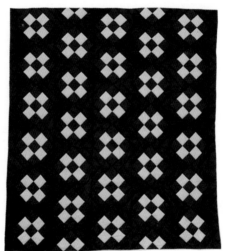

5190392

6190392

7190392

1190392 – BLOOMING BULBS; 50" x 50"; white background, pink sashing, flowers in pink, mauve, lavender, purple, yellow, gold, peach & dark green; prewashed cotton; made in Pennsylvania in 1986; machine appliqued & quilted; Mountain Mist low-loft batting, quilted by the block & assembled w/sashing on front & back. $172.00

2190392 – WEDDING RING; 88" x 108"; black w/rose & green flower & leaves, corners are black & rose, off-white background; cotton with cotton/polyester backing; made in Kansas in 1991; machine pieced, hand quilted; cotton/polyester batting; double binding; quilted around each piece with a flower design in the middle. $460.00

3190392 – JAPANESE GARDEN; 50" x 50"; dark rose w/cream & rose print; 100% cotton; made in Washington in 1987; machine pieced, hand quilted; polyester batting; the quilt gets its name from the large floral print fabric (imported from Japan) used in the quilt. $1,725.00

4190392 – MARTHA WASHINGTON FLOWER GARDEN; 98" x 102"; multicolored, set together w/white; cottons; made in Alabama in 1989; completely made by hand, quilted on each side of seam; polyester batting, white sheet lining, white quilt binding. $575.00

5190392 – DIAMOND PATTERN; 81" x 91"; emerald green, royal blue & cream; cotton & cotton/polyester; made in Alabama in 1989; hand pieced & quilted; Mountain Mist batting. $345.00

6190392 – LOVE RING VARIATION; 90" x 96"; black & white; cotton/polyester; made in Missouri in 1990; machine pieced & quilted; polyester batting. $230.00

7190392 – LITTLE PINE TREE (original design); 46" x 51"; variety of greens; cotton w/a few cotton/poly blends; made in Illinois in 1990; machine pieced & quilted drawings of birds, animals, trees, etc.; polyester batting; began w/a simple tree design & ended up a park. $230.00

1010692

2010692

3010692

4010692

5010692

6010692

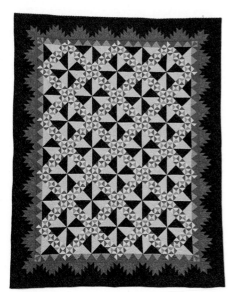

7010692

1010692 – LOVE ROSES; 61" x 73"; dusty roses, burgundies, green, black; cotton; made in Iowa in 1991; hand made; poly low-loft batting; made for Labor of Love Contest, juried into show; Best of Show winner at an Omaha, Nebraska show, hanging sleeve, extensive quilting. $805.00

2010692 – SUNFLOWER; 86" x 96"; blues, country blue, white, dark blue, reds, green stems & leaves, green binding; cotton prints; made in Indiana in 1991; all hand made; polyester batting. $805.00

3010692 – GRANDMOTHER'S FLOWER GARDEN; 93" x 93"; assorted solids with solid white path; cotton blends; made in Kentucky in 1991; hand pieced & quilted; polyester batting; hand quilted around each piece. $460.00

4010692 – LOG CABIN; 79" x 91"; brown prints with unbleached muslin; all prewashed cotton fabrics; made in South Carolina in 1991; one-step piecing & quilting by machine (quilt as you go method); polyester low-loft batting; double edge binding. $276.00

5010692 – DAHLIA; 70" x 88"; pink, purple, off-white; 100% cotton; made in California 1991; machine pieced, hand quilted; poly batt; bright colors & unusual fabric combinations. $690.00

6010692 – TREE OF LIFE; 92" x 96"; white, country blue, yellow, some reds, green stems & leaves, brown tree & leaves, green binding; all cotton prints; made in 1991 in Indiana; all hand made, polyester batting. $1150.00

7010692 – PINWHEELS; 68" x 82"; aubergine, celery, periwinkle, lilac, cream, green & rose; all cotton; made in California in 1992; cotton classic batting; large pinwheel blocks sashed with rows of small pinwheels, border of mystery mountains, backing of batik in paisley print of same colors; all fabrics on front are softly figured prints. $345.00

1020692

2020692

3020692

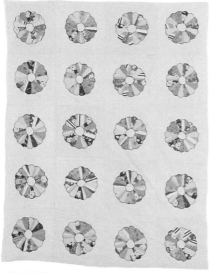

4020692

5020692

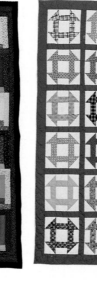

6020692

1020692 – DRESDEN PLATE; 86" x 100"; shades of mauve & burgundy on cream background; all cotton top with poly/cotton backing & batting; made in Kansas in 1984; machine pieced, hand quilted; mitered borders, double binding; blue ribbon winner at county fair. $345.00

2020692 – NO NAME; 16" x 32"; mauve, pink & aqua; cotton blend fabrics; made in Nebraska in 1992; machine strip pieced, hand quilted; poly fil batt; used as table runner or wallhanging, hanging sleeve on back. $60.00

3020692 – TULIPS; 107" x 104"; white background with mauve embroidery; cotton; made in Maryland in 1991; hand quilted & embroidered; Mountain Mist batting; washed once to remove quilt lines. $489.00

4020692 – FIRST EFFORTS – DRESDEN PLATES; 72" x 89"; multicolored feed sack prints, background solid natural feed sacks, muslin backing; cottons, muslin, black embroidery floss; top made in early 1930's, finished 1991; hand pieced, quilted & appliqued; batting is "outing" flannel; top made by owner's mother when a young girl, quilting by owner (a quilt teacher). $345.00

5020692 – LOG CABIN; 94" x 102"; blue on blue, navy, blue lining; cotton; made in Alabama in 1991; machine pieced, hand quilted on each side of seam; poly batt, sheet lining, light-to-dark print. $402.00

6020692 – CHURN DASH; 73" x 88"; multicolor prints/solids, white, med.-to-dark blue, white backing; 1960's fabrics/broadcloth; made in Arkansas, blocks made in mid 1960's, finished in 1991; machine pieced, hand quilted; poly batt, double bias binding, quilted hearts in border. $230.00

7020692 – LOG CABIN SCRAP VARIATION; 86" x 102"; multicolored w/white backing; cotton fabrics; made in Iowa in 1989; completely hand made quilt; Mountain Mist Traditional Loft batting; bright colors. $316.00

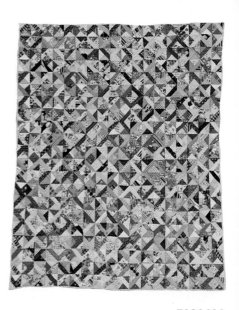

7020692

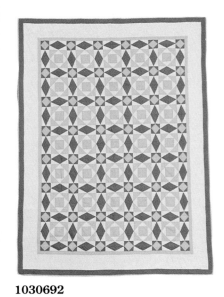

1030692

2030692

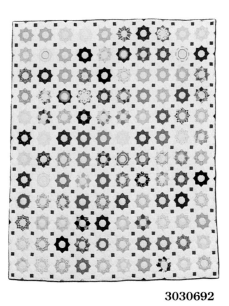

3030692

4030692

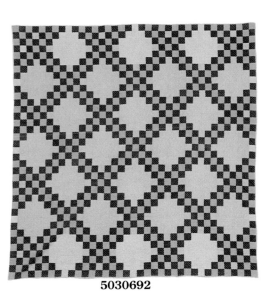

5030692

6030692

7030692

1030692 – STORM AT SEA; 72" x 84"; beige, off-white, gray & beige, some dotted material; cotton; made in 1988 in Florida; machine pieced, hand quilted; border has feathered quilting plus background quilting. $460.00

2030692 – DRUNKARD'S PATH; 86" x 94"; burgundy & white; broadcloth; made in Arkansas in 1990; hand pieced & quilted; double bias binding, polyester batting. $230.00

3030692 – FLOWER GARDEN STAR; 78" x 92"; assorted prints & solids, white background, green border; cotton & cotton/polyester blends; made in Arkansas in 1989; hand pieced & quilted; polyester batting, double bias binding. $270.00

4030692 – ZIG-ZAG 1992; 68" x 86"; multicolored center, dark blue inner border, light blue wide outer border, pale pink & white print binding; 100% cotton; made in Illinois in 1992; machine pieced & quilted; polyester low-loft batting; variety of solid colors, circular echo quilting in border. $230.00

5030692 – IRISH CHAIN; 86" x 86"; pink, green & orange; cottons; made c. 1900; maker unknown; hand quilted; excellent condition, unusual combination of colors with orange & green "chain" on pink background. $299.00

6030692 – OHIO ROSE; 74" x 90"; blue & green on beige; cotton & polyester with cotton backing; made in Ohio in 1992; hand quilted & appliqued; quilting closer than most. $518.00

7030692 – CRAZY QUILT; 79" x 88"; all colors, light blue border; cotton/polyester blends; made in Georgia in 1990; machine pieced, hand embroidered, quilted & hemmed. $402.00

43

1040692

2040692

3040692

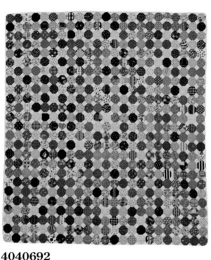

4040692

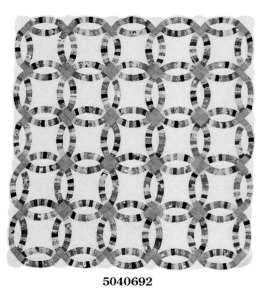

5040692

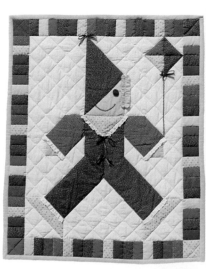

6040692

1040692 – DOUBLE WEDDING RING; 30" x 30"; blue background print with dusty pink flowers; cotton/polyester fabrics; made in Missouri in 1991; machine pieced, hand quilted; Dacron™ batting, off-white background, tabs attached for hanging, heart quilting design. $55.00

2040692 – DOUBLE IRISH CHAIN; 88" x 108"; peach & sea foam; cotton; made in Pennsylvania in 1992; machine pieced, hand quilted; double edge binding; polyester batting. $518.00

3040692 – MEXICAN STAR VARIATION; 84" x 92"; medium & dark blue, pink, off-white; 100% cotton; made in New York in 1991; machine pieced & quilted; center medallion on muslin background with 6" calico border; piecing has outline quilting, the muslin is embellished with feathered plumes & circles; backing is 50/50 polycotton. $402.00

4040692 – COBBLESTONES; 86" x 94"; multicolored country prints with muslin, muslin binding, light blue backing; cotton/polyester; made in Ohio in 1989; hand pieced & quilted; quilted by the piece; Mountain Mist polyester batting; pillow included. $489.00

5040692 – DOUBLE WEDDING RING; 86" x 86"; multicolored prints, white background, white lining; cotton & cotton blends; made in Virginia in 1992; machine pieced, hand quilted; Poly-fil extra loft batting, double bias binding. $288.00

6040692 – CLOWN (original design); 34" x 41"; red, blue, yellow, green calicoes & dots on muslin, trimmed w/eyelet, rickrack & ribbon; all cotton; made in Pennsylvania in 1991; machine pieced, hand quilted; quilt appears in Feb/March issue of *Stitch 'N Sew Quilts*. $144.00

7040692 – BEARS PAW; 48" x 48"; five shades of blue w/dark, dusty rose; 100% prewashed fabrics; made in New York in 1990; machine pieced, hand quilted; paws quilted in the ditch, rest is heavily quilted in rope pattern; repro. feed & grain sack on unbleached muslin for backing. $259.00

7040692

44

1050692

2050692

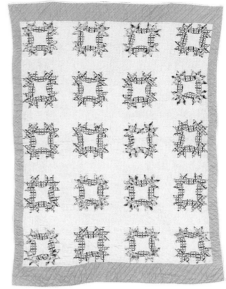

3050692

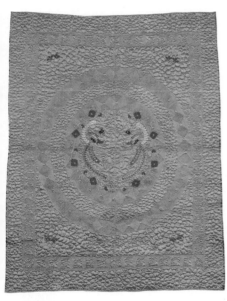

4050692

5050692

6050692

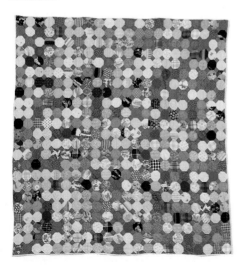

7050692

1050692 – GRAPE BASKET; 90" x 103"; blue & white; cotton; made in Kentucky in 1991; hand pieced & quilted; feather wreath quilting, chevron quilting on border 1" apart. $345.00

2050692 – DOUBLE WEDDING RING; 76" x 90"; multicolored prints on pale blue background, white seamless backing; cotton & cotton/polyester blends; made in Kentucky in 1991; hand pieced & quilted; Mountain Mist polyester batting. $489.00

3050692 – 1950's PINEAPPLE TOP; 74" x 96"; orange & yellow on white background w/mint border; cotton; made in Missouri in 1989; hand pieced top made in 1950's (all hand sewn). $316.00

4050692 – KOREAN MARRIAGE QUILT; 62" x 79"; gold & green; made in Seoul, South Korea in 1962; quilt was bought in a little shop on a side street in Seoul, purchased as a gift for the owner's mother, never used, has been in storage since then until last year; price set by certified appraiser. $1,955.00

5050692 – STAR WITHIN A STAR; 47" x 58"; browns, rusts & golds; 100% cotton; made in Idaho in 1985; machine pieced, hand quilted; 1st place wallhanging at the Eastern Idaho State Fair in 1985 & a 1st place small pieced category at the Tribune Home & Garden Show in Salt Lake City. $150.00

6050692 – LONE STAR; 93" x 110"; various blue prints on cream background; cotton & cotton/polyester blends with muslin backing; made by Amish in Pennsylvania in 1989 (never used); hand quilted. $448.00

7050692 – OZARK COBBLESTONES; 82" x 86"; predominantly blue, off-white backing & binding, variety of colors; cotton & cotton blends; made in Arkansas in 1991; hand pieced & quilted; polyester batting, double bias batting. $259.00

1060692

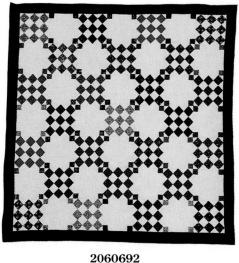

2060692

3060692

4060692

5060692

6060692

1060692 – PASSION FLOWER; 32" circular; coral, Chinese red, green, violet, maroon, mustard, blue; cotton blends & hand dyed cottons; made in Colorado in 1991; hand & machine pieced, hand quilted with metallic thread, bead embellishment; bold jungle print with hand dyed fabrics give a new look to the Mariner's Compass pattern; polyester batting. $288.00

2060692 – CHECKERBOARD; 78" x 80"; top made in 1950's by unknown maker in Alabama; hand quilted in 1991, machine pieced; 100% cotton; feathered circle quilting design, pieced blocks outlined with ¼" quilting. $575.00

3060692 – ROMAN STRIPE; 57" x 72"; pink, black & bright multicolored; silks with sateen backing; made in 1920's in New York; maker unknown; hand pieced in strips, set with strips of black & pink print silk; very thin batting; some silks from men's ties; tied quilt (ties invisible). $345.00

4060692 – TRELLIS ROSE; 82" x 98"; mauve, rose & white; cotton; made in Kansas in 1991; machine pieced, hand quilted & appliqued; Mountain Mist batting, mitered corners, double binding. $460.00

5060692 – SUNBONNET SUE & OVERALL BILL; 45" x 74"; red check, white blocks, red & blue calicoes; cotton; hand quilted in red thread, machine appliqued; red check backing. $201.00

6060692 – ENCIRCLED TULIP; 88" x 100"; shades of country blue, white & mauve; cotton top w/cotton/poly backing; made in Kansas in 1991; machine pieced, hand quilted & appliqued tulips; tulips have a mauve center w/blue on the outside; double binding mitered corners. $345.00

7060692 – FLYING BATS; 90" x 100"; turquoise, black & off-white with rose accent; cotton; made in Oklahoma in 1991; machine pieced, hand quilted; Fairfield's Extra Loft batting; centered flowers in each block are made of older fabric. $575.00

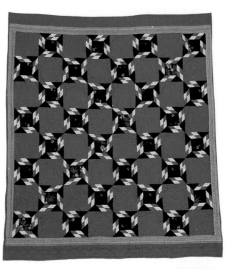

7060692

46

1070692

2070692

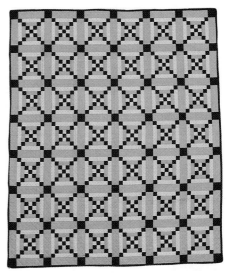

3070692

4070692

5070692

6070692

7070692

1070692 – FLORAL LOVE RING; 46" x 46"; blue background, peach & pink flowers, tan floral border; 100% cottons; made in Indiana in 1991; hand quilted; polyester batting, Victorian floral print set Drunkard's Path style to form a Love Ring. $115.00

2070692 – SAN DIEGO SUNSHINE; 36" x 48"; coral & blue prints; mostly cotton with some poly blends; made in California in 1991; machine pieced, hand quilted; Mountain Mist regular polyester batting; half of the blocks frame rabbit pictures. $60.00

3070692 – ALABAMA; 84" x 108"; chocolate, peach & cream, muslin back; prewashed 100% cotton; made in Illinois in 1988; machine pieced, hand quilted; Mountain Mist batting; excellent quilting. $431.00

4070692 – PINWHEEL; 27" x 27"; many shades of brown, beige & rust; 100% cotton; made in Pennsylvania in 1988; machine pieced, hand quilted; Pellon fleece batting; inspired by Martha McCloskey workshop; border is quilted in tiny pinwheel-type curved contraptions. $126.00

5070692 – TRIP AROUND THE WORLD; 88" x 88"; different shades of green; mostly cotton fabrics; hand pieced & quilted. $345.00

6070692 – DOUBLE IRISH CHAIN; 40" x 50"; pink & blue, off-white background with pink & blue print; cotton; made in Alabama in 1989; machine pieced, hand quilted; polyester batting, lambs quilted in background areas. $109.00

7070692 – PINE BURR BLOCKS; 68" x 88"; mixed colors; cotton, cotton muslin back; made in Arkansas in 1991; machine pieced & quilted; hand made binding, machine quilted in a scroll pattern. $150.00

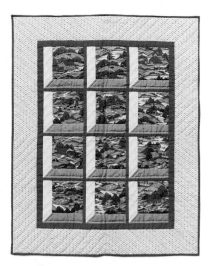

1080692

2080692

3080692

4080692

5080692

6080692

1080692 – ATTIC WINDOWS; 31" x 37"; maroon, white, blue-gray with farmland window scenes; all cotton; made in South Carolina in 1991; machine pieced, hand quilted; windows depict various colored farm scenes; tiny duck print on borders; muslin backing; maroon binding. $155.00

2080692 – TRIP AROUND THE WORLD; 72" x 85"; multicolored scrap quilt with blues, greens, creams, reds, golds & navy; cotton & cotton/polyester blends; hand pieced by three generations of quilters, hand quilted & bound; made in Virginia in late 1980's; made of 1⅞" squares, set on the diagonal. $288.00

3080692 – FALLING LEAVES; 82" x 90"; cream, earth tone leaves, reversible—other side is rust; cotton/polyester blend; made in Illinois in 1977; hand pieced, quilted & appliqued; polyester high-loft batting; leaves are cascading down on cream colored side. $460.00

4080692 – STAR TRIP; 82" x 96"; navy & beige; 100% cotton; made in Minnesota in 1991; hand quilted; Mountain Mist batting; a Trip Around the World with a center star & 4 more stars set in each corner; lots of quilting. $345.00

5080692 – PLAIN REVERSIBLE QUILT; 96" x 107"; off-white, beige, unbleached muslin; cotton/polyester; made in Illinois in 1992; hand quilted; polyester Super Fluff batting; reversible quilt. $230.00

6080692 – SUMMER GARDEN; 41" x 40"; browns, tan, greens, orange, black & gray; 100% cotton; made in New York in 1991; hand appliqued & quilted, machine strip pieced; garden with vegetables, cats, a rabbit & scarecrow; polyester batting; hanging sleeve on back. $201.00

7080692 – LOG CABIN; 70" x 90"; red, white & blue; cotton; made in New York in 1988; completely hand made; Mountain Mist batting. $345.00

7080692

1090692

2090692

3090692

4090692

5090692

6090692

7090692

1090692 – APPLIQUE; 42" x 55"; white, yellow, blue "Mickey Mouse"; cotton & polyester fabrics; made in Illinois in 1992; hand quilted & appliqued; Dacron™ batting. $55.00

2090692 – TREASURE; 98" x 98"; flower print, soft wine, soft green, off-white muslin backing; all cotton materials; all hand made; made in New Jersey in 1991; maker found the pattern in an old book, the arrangement of the blocks (12") gives the effect of the colors going in rows; Fairfield Traditional batting, lace. $862.00

3090692 – TULIPS & HEARTS APPLIQUE; 79" x 106"; green, pink, purple, blue, off-white; 100% cotton; made in California in 1991; hand quilted & appliqued; polyester batting, a secondary pattern comes out of the placement of the blocks. $690.00

4090692 – MORNING STAR; 89" x 102"; burgundy, forest green & cream; cotton; made in Wisconsin in 1992; machine pieced & quilted; Dacron™ polyester batting. $288.00

5090692 – LONE STAR; 94" x 110"; dominant colors dark navy to light-dark, burgundy shaded to light, off-white background; 100% cotton print; made in 1991 in Missouri; machine pieced, hand quilted; polyester batting. $402.00

6090692 – RISING STAR; 46" x 67"; red, blue & brown calicoes, cream background; cotton (the red is poly/cotton blend); made in Iowa in 1989; machine pieced, hand quilted; polyester batting, overall design is stars within stars. $230.00

7090692 – BRAVE NEW ALBUM; 55" x 58"; predominantly teal blue background & borders with various red accents; cotton & cotton blends; made in Colorado in 1991; machine pieced, hand quilted; album block variation, off-centered medallion created by varying background colors; chocolate brown backing, Hobbs poly black batting, sleeve for hanging. $345.00

49

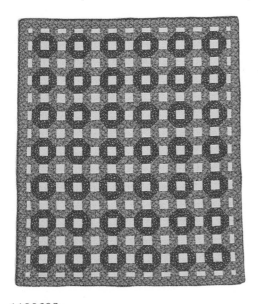

1100692

2100692

3100692

4100692

5100692

6100692

1100692 – COMING HOME; 77" x 89"; blue-green print, maroon floral & cream print squares, muslin back; 100% cotton; made in Illinois in 1988; machine pieced, hand quilted; quilted on both sides of seam. $345.00

2100692 – UNTITLED SQUARES; 34" x 50"; assorted prints on top, off-white back; polyester/cotton blend fabrics; made in 1991 in Pennsylvania; machine pieced, hand tied; polyester batting. $70.00

3100692 – CROSSROADS TO JERICHO; 75" x 71"; indigo, mauve, yellow with sprigged white, calico background; cotton calicoes; made c. 1900 in Pennsylvania; hand made; maker's name on back; good condition with some fading. $431.00

4100692 – GEESE IN FLIGHT; 80" x 90"; aqua with multicolored prints & solids; cotton & cotton/polyester blends; made in Ohio in 1991; machine pieced, hand quilted; beige, aqua & pink print cotton backing, aqua binding; polyester batting. $345.00

5100692 – YO-YO; 45" x 68"; multicolored prints bordered with solid yellow; cotton; made by quilt owner's mother c. 1940 in Arkansas Ozarks; completely hand made. $230.00

6100692 – NAVAHO; 92" x 103"; brown, peach, green, off-white; polyester/cotton blends; made in Ohio in 1991; machine pieced, hand quilted. $460.00

7100692 – BUTTERFLY QUILT; 88" x 108"; country blue, off-white, backing off-white; cotton & cotton/polyester blends; made in Illinois in 1991; machine pieced, hand quilted & appliqued; polyester batting; bound with points. $316.00

7100692

1110692

2110692

3110692

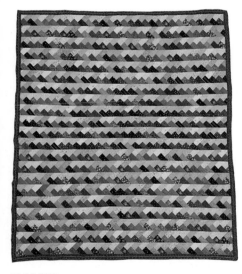

4110692

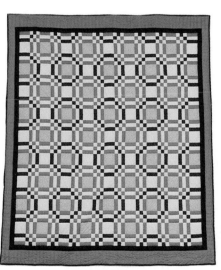

5110692

6110692

7110692

1110692 – LONE STAR; 40" x 40"; peach & greens; cotton; made in Washington in 1992; machine pieced, hand quilted; Cotton Classic batting. $172.00

2110692 – THIRD COW ON THE LEFT/WATERWHEEL; 77" x 89"; brown & beige; 100% cotton top, unbleached muslin backing, only one piece of polyester; made in Indiana in 1990; machine pieced, hand tied with crochet yarn; Mountain Mist regular loft batting; this quilt was honored to play the part of a cow in the Brown County Playhouse production of *Quilters* by Indiana U., Summer 1990; a pleasant knock-about utility quilt. $250.00

3110692 – SILVER ANNIVERSARY; 78" x 92"; white with "silver" gray print; cotton/polyester 50% blend fabric; machine pieced, hand quilted; made in Texas in 1990; can be used "as is" or the names of couple added in center black with anniversary date by liquid embroidery pen or marker; silver metallic fabric paint used on wedding bells, rings & writing. $230.00

4110692 – FRIENDSHIP BRAID; 84" x 104"; multicolored; cotton; made in Illinois in 1992; machine pieced, hand quilted; polyester batting, this quilt would blend in any decor. $345.00

5110692 – IRIS JIG; 83" x 96"; blue prints & solids with white; cotton/polyester; made in Missouri in 1991; machine pieced, hand quilted; polyester batting. $345.00

6110692 – BROKEN STAR LOG CABIN; 84" x 105"; seven values of blue, white; cotton prints & solid; made in Ohio in 1992; machine pieced, hand quilted; double fabric bound, much hand quilting; polyester batting. $500.00

7110692 – LOG CABIN; 100" x 100"; multicolored quilt with off-white lining; made in 1990 in Tennessee; machine pieced, hand quilted; polyester batting. $345.00

51

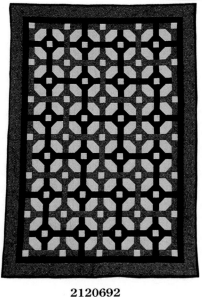

1120692

2120692

3120692

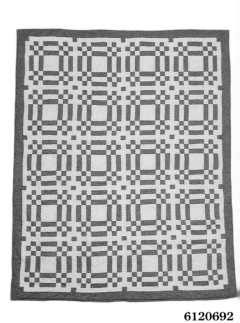

4120692

5120692

6120692

1120692 – LOG CABIN; 90" x 109"; red, brown, beige; cotton & cotton/polyester blend; made in Illinois in 1992; machine pieced, hand quilted; Dacron™ batting. $230.00

2120692 – TILE PUZZLE; 63" x 86"; background is light gray with gray & black design; 100% cotton; made in 1991 in Wisconsin; machine pieced, hand quilted; fabrics were chosen to give the impression of granite & marble to reflect the title of the puzzle. $172.00

3120692 – MARINER'S COMPASS; 78" x 84"; mulberry, off-white, pink; cotton/polyester blends; made in Wisconsin in 1991; machine pieced; machine quilted using soft monofilament nylon thread, using the heirloom machine quilting techniques developed by H. Hargrove; polyester batting, seamless preshrunk muslin backing. $201.00

4120692 – LONE STAR; 59" x 59"; background rusts & cream, star in pastels; cotton; made in Wisconsin in 1991; machine pieced, machine & hand quilted; Mountain Mist polyester batting; hanging sleeve on back. $316.00

5120692 – VARIABLE STAR; 74" x 94"; multicolors with pink stripping & green binding, green backing; all cottons; unknown maker, probably made in 1930's; machine pieced, hand quilted; a cotton quilt with cotton batting, 48 different stars for the 48 states; good condition. $288.00

6120692 – CORNER NINE PATCH; 87" x 103"; blue & white; cotton/polyester; made in Missouri in 1991; machine pieced & quilted; polyester batting. $230.00

7120692 – TWIN STAR; 30" x 30"; rose, teal, black, pale green; cotton; made in Minnesota in 1991; hand pieced, hand quilted; polyester batting, sleeve on back for hanging or can be used as table cover. $86.00

7120692

1130692

2130692 ➡

3130692

4130692

5130692

6130692

7130692

1130692 – SPECTRUM MAZE; 70" x 70"; multicolored shades of red, yellow, blue, green; predominantly solid colors, some prints; all cotton pieced top, black/white cotton/poly backing; made in California in 1990; machine pieced, hand quilted, some hand applique; center section has crosshatch quilting, corner edge panels are quilted in a waved sunburst design, multicolored triangles are hand appliqued. $460.00

2130692 – OCEAN WAVES; 82" x 102"; unbleached muslin background, scrap fabric triangles; cotton & cotton/polyester blend fabrics; made in Indiana in 1991; machine pieced, machine quilted following Ocean Waves pattern; 100% cotton batting. $201.00

3130692 – CHEVRON; 80" x 103"; country blues; cotton; made in Ohio in 1991; machine pieced & quilted in clamshell design; polyester batting. $196.00

4130692 – STARS & STRIPES; 74" x 90"; multicolored stars set together with white; red, white & blue flags with stars on backing; cotton/poly blends; made in Kentucky, top made in 1987, machine quilted in 1992; hand & machine pieced; quilt can be used on either side. $288.00

5130692 – FLOWER BASKET; 86" x 102"; blue & white; polyester/cotton blends; machine pieced, hand quilted & embroidered; polyester batting; original flower design; quilted seam by seam. $196.00

6130692 – CROSSROADS; 76" x 87"; multicolored print triangles & solid rectangles, center squares muslin, all colors, light blue backing; cotton/polyester; made in Ohio in 1988; hand pieced & quilted; polyester batting. $489.00

7130692 – VIRGINIA LILY; 82" x 94"; pink & green on white; cotton; made in Illinois in 1991; machine pieced, hand quilted; polyester batting. $276.00

1140692

2140692

3140692

4140692

5140692

6140692

1140692 – SUMMER STARS; 86" x 104"; solid pastel green broadcloth, varied cotton print; cotton; made in Tennessee in 1991; hand pieced & quilted; polyester batting, home-dyed sheeting for lining. $460.00

2140692 – DRESDEN PLATE; 92" x 112"; off-white muslin backing with dark green stripping, rusts & greens; cottons; made in Idaho in 1989; machine pieced & appliqued with satin stitch, hand quilted; polyester batting. $690.00

3140692 – LOG CABIN VARIATION; 76" x 76"; blues & oranges with blue as backing brought to the front to form the binding; cottons; made in Kansas, blocks made in the 1930's, quilt finished in 1980's; hand & machine pieced, hand quilted; lightweight polyester batting; unusual to see orange in 1930's blocks! $166.00

4140692 – COLORADO LOG CABIN; 68" x 86"; shades of blue with white backing (reversible quilt); cotton; made in Michigan in 1991; machine pieced, hand quilted; polyester Mountain Mist batting, double binding, quilted border. $402.00

5140692 – CUBIC TURTLES; 54" x 54"; hot pink, cranberry, gray & black; 100% cotton Jenny Beyer fabrics; made in Illinois in 1992; machine pieced, hand quilted (interesting pieced back); Blue Ribbon cotton batting; permanent rod pocket matches back of quilt, black binding "frames" the wall quilt. $345.00

6140692 – JACOB'S LADDER; 89" x 101"; blue & mauve with white; cotton/polyester; made in Missouri in 1991; machine pieced, hand quilted; polyester batting. $230.00

7140692 – DUTCH ROSE; 90" x 102"; multicolored; cotton/polyester; made in Missouri in 1991; machine pieced, hand quilted; polyester batting. $345.00

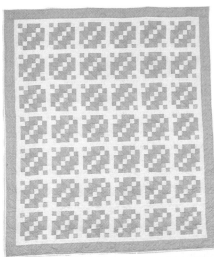

7140692

54

1150692

2150692

3150692

4150692

5150692

6150692

7150692

1150692 – IRISH CHAIN; 84" x 104"; blue & rose; cotton; made in Texas in 1991; machine pieced, hand quilted; feather heart quilting; Mountain Mist batting. $345.00

2150692 – LOG CABIN STAR; 49" x 63"; Christmas reds, greens & white; cotton; made in Alabama in 1991; machine pieced & quilted; polyester batting; backing is white Christmas fabric with holly leaves. $144.00

3150692 – LONE STAR; 94" x 100"; blue with white fill; cotton/polyester; made in Missouri in 1991; machine pieced, hand quilted; polyester batting. $345.00

4150692 – STAR BRIGHT; 43" x 55"; reds, black accents, unbleached muslin background & backing; cotton; made in Virginia in 1991; machine pieced, hand quilted; low-loft poly batting; variable star blocks set on point, single cable quilted on border; lap quilt or wallhanging. $230.00

5150692 – LOG CABIN – BARNRAISING; 120" x 120"; beige & earth tones, shades of rust & brown; cotton; made in Missouri in 1989; machine pieced, hand quilted; polyester high fill batting. $690.00

6150692 – SHADOW RAIL; 41" x 52"; brown, burgundy, red & cream; cotton; made in Montana in 1984; machine pieced, hand quilted; polyester batting, sleeve for hanging. $86.00

7150692 – DAISY CHAIN; 82" x 92"; burgundy stars & border, multicolored, muslin background (off-white); mostly cottons (a few polyester blends); made in Michigan in 1991; machine pieced, hand quilted in burgundy thread; Hi-loft Fairfield batting, double binding. $483.00

55

1160692

2160692

3160692

4160692

6160692

5160692

7160692

1160692 – TRIPLE RAIL; 60" x 60"; pink, blue & black, black backing; 100% prewashed cotton fabrics; made in Ohio in 1989; machine pieced, hand quilted in black with 1" diagonal grid & floral design; 100% cotton batting, black thread, double binding. $402.00

2160692 – BROKEN STAR; 28" x 28"; black, peach, blue; all cotton; made in South Carolina in 1990; machine pieced, hand quilted; Mountain Mist batting. $110.00

3160692 – FIFTY-FOUR FORTY OR FIGHT; 90" x 100"; white, black, red; 100% cotton; made in Minnesota in 1991; machine pieced, hand quilted; Mountain Mist batting. $345.00

4160692 – TENNESSEE RAINBOW; 48" x 57"; rainbow colors; cottons & cotton blends; made in California in 1988; machine pieced, hand quilted; extensive quilting makes this quilt durable enough for functional use as well as decorative use; has won awards. $518.00

5160692 – POSTAGE STAMP; 94" x 94"; multicolored, 4422 blocks arranged with darks & lights to incorporate a patriotic message which can be read at a distance; cotton/polyester blend fabrics; made in Oregon in 1991; machine pieced, hand quilted; pieced during Desert Storm. $402.00

6160692 – GIANT DAHLIA; 62" x 62"; shades of dusty greens & rusty reds; cotton; made in Minnesota in 1991; machine pieced, hand quilted; French fold bias binding; backing is light green print (the same as binding), petals are appliqued to center of dahlia; Mountain Mist light batting; coordinated St. Nicole cotton fabrics. $288.00

7160692 – LEMOYNE STAR; 48" x 48"; olive green background with dark green border; blue, green & hot pink stars; cotton; made in Georgia in 1991; machine pieced, hand quilted; polyester batting, heavily quilted. $230.00

56

1170692

2170692

3170692

4170692

5170692 ➡

7170692

6170692

1170692 – THREE PATCH; 86" x 102"; green & white; cotton & cotton/polyester blends; made in Idaho in 1990–1992; machine pieced, hand quilted; polyester batting. $460.00

2170692 – VASE OF FLOWERS; 75" x 75"; blue, white, cranberry; cotton & cotton/polyester fabrics; made in Connecticut in 1989; machine pieced, hand quilted; double bias bound, polyester batting. $299.00

3170692 – CORNERS IN THE CABINS; 23" x 23"; wine, blue, ecru, mauve; cotton fabrics; made in Nebraska in 1991; machine pieced, hand quilted; triangle corners are incorporated with a unique technique which leaves the long edge free…frequently called "toe catchers"; hanging sleeve. $70.00

4170692 – DOGWOOD; 86" x 108"; rose with green & white corners; all cotton with cotton/polyester backing; made in Kansas in 1991; machine pieced, hand quilted & appliqued; mitered corners, double binding. $391.00

5170692 – TRIANGLE TWIST; 84" x 100"; earth tones; 100% cotton; made in Alabama in 1991; machine pieced, completely free-hand machine quilted; Hobbs Bonded batting. $575.00

6170692 – GIRAFFE & ELEPHANT; 38" x 51"; green, yellow & blue print (child's); cotton & cotton/polyester; machine pieced & quilted, hand embroidered & appliqued; made in Wisconsin in 1991; polyester batting. $60.00

7170692 – CHURN DASH; 87" x 94"; chocolate brown print with white background print; all cotton; made in Tennessee in 1988; machine pieced, hand quilted; 9" blocks, matching binding, polyester batting, bleached muslin backing. $264.00

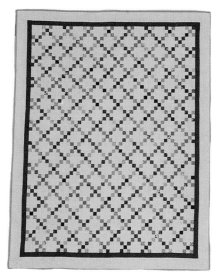

1180692

2180692

3180692

4180692

5180692

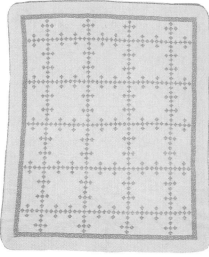

6180692

1180692 – SINGLE IRISH CHAIN; 84" x 106"; multicolored 1½" squares against a muslin background, country blue, white pin dot back; prewashed 100% cotton fabrics; made in Illinois in 1991; machine pieced, hand quilted. $460.00

2180692 – SAMPLER; 48" x 48"; blue & dusty mauve using border prints to enhance the design; 100% cotton; made in Florida in 1988; hand pieced & quilted; heavily quilted. $259.00

3180692 – SAILBOATS; 42" x 42"; pastel colors with blue polka dot & plaid yellow sashings; cotton; made in Georgia/Maine in 1992; machine pieced, hand quilted; pastel sailboats on mint background, mint binding; four pieced triangles make up backing. $201.00

4180692 – LOG CABIN; 41" x 41" & 20" x 20"; brown, beige with accent of rust; cotton & cotton/polyester; machine pieced & quilted; made in New York in 1992; a companion piece is included – both pieces have a sleeve for easy hanging; polyester batting; sold as a set. $155.00

5180692 – WINDMILL; 81" x 96"; bright red, red print, red polka dot & white; cotton/polyester blend fabrics & cotton; made in Missouri in 1988 (quilt never used); machine pieced & quilted in a leafy vine design, backing solid red. $201.00

6180692 – SINGLE IRISH CHAIN; 90" x 104"; green with peach flowers, light peach print background; cotton; made in California in 1991; machine pieced, hand quilted; polyester batting; quilted intricately with feather wreath design. $518.00

7180692 – GRANDMOTHER'S FLOWER GARDEN; 69" x 70"; white background with various colored flowers; cotton; made in Pennsylvania in 1960's; hand pieced & quilted. $230.00

7180692

1190692

2190692

3190692

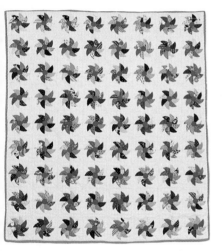

4190692

5190692

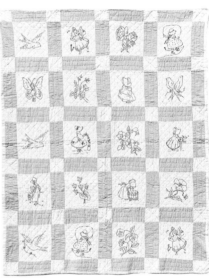

6190692

7190692

1190692 – MARTHA WASHINGTON FLOWER GARDEN; 80" x 104"; multicolors & tan, tan border, white background; cotton; made in Iowa in 1989; machine pieced, hand quilted; poly batt. $316.00

2190692 – FLOWER GARDEN; 60" x 75"; blue, pink, yellow, shades of green, white background; cotton; made in Missouri in 1991; hand quilted & embroidered, machine & hand quilted; comes with matching wallhanging 36" x 36". $805.00

3190692 – CELTIC SQUARES; 84" x 98"; pastel pink & green w/white background w/pink & green paisley print; cotton & cotton blends; made in Ohio in 1991; hand pieced & quilted; poly batt. $184.00

4190692 – PINWHEEL; 81" x 96"; pinwheel made with medium blue center, each blade with multicolored prints, medium blue binding; cotton/polyester; made in Ohio in 1991; hand pieced & quilted; quilted by the piece; polyester batting. $489.00

5190692 – PERSUASION (original design); 100" x 100"; peachy pinks, terra cotta, teal green, black; cotton; made in Idaho in 1991; machine pieced, hand quilted & bound; Fairfield Extra Loft poly batt, double batted, delicate butterflies & flowers in warm shades of rose & teal against black background, outer edge has extra batting for a corded effect; a dozen silky tassels. $900.00

6190692 – EMBROIDERED CRIB QUILT; 47" x 56"; white background, red embroidery; cotton; made in 1940's by unknown maker; machine pieced, hand quilted & embroidered w/red thread; cotton batt; has embroidered children, flowers & tiny red & white gingham sashing. $288.00

7190692 – PUMPKIN PATCH; 83" x 93"; multicolored 9-patch with cream color framed with cream, green & natural calico, a touch of red buds; cotton & poly cotton fabrics; made in Illinois in 1992; machine pieced, hand quilted; polyester batting. $276.00

1010992

2010992

3010992

4010992

5010992

6010992

7010992

1010992 – BUTTERFLY; 78" x 89"; multicolored butterflies, off-white background & backing, green sashing; cotton; made in 1930's in Missouri; hand appliqued with buttonhole stitch, machine assembled, hand quilted; cotton batting, has a few age spots. $288.00

2010992 – SECRET ARBOR; 45" x 45"; white, blue, black, red, solid red background; 100% cotton; made in New York in 1990; all hand pieced & quilted; polyester batting, sleeve on back for hanging. $316.00

3010992 – WEDDING RING; 98" x 102"; brown print with rust & green corners on a cream background; all cotton with poly/cotton backing; made in Kansas in 1991; machine pieced, hand quilted; polyester batting, has lots of quilting in center, double binding. $448.00

4010992 – IRIS; 88" x 94"; orchid, pink, yellow, purple, red, green, green binding, white background; cotton blends; made in Indiana in 1990; all hand made, polyester batting. $920.00

5010992 – SCHOOLHOUSE & IRISH CHAIN; 42" x 42"; red, green, white print; cotton; made in Illinois in 1991; machine pieced, hand quilted; backing is tiny apple print on green, polyester batting. $178.00

6010992 – FOUR PATCH CHAIN; 82" x 100"; medium blue, navy & white; 100% cotton; made in Wisconsin in 1990; machine pieced, hand quilted; polyester batting; matching navy print backing, fabrics are preshrunk. $218.00

7010992 – LONE STAR; 41" x 41"; mauve & blue with cream background; cotton/polyester; made in Missouri in 1991; machine pieced, hand quilted; polyester batting. $86.00

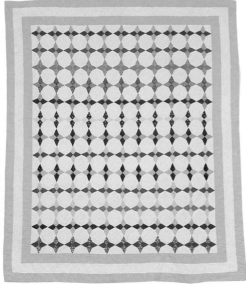

1020992

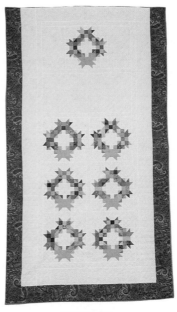

2020992

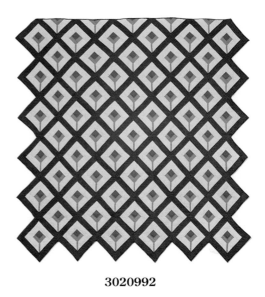

3020992

4020992

5020992

6020992

1020992 – PONTIAC STAR; 92" x 102"; multicolored stars w/yellow border on white background; 100% cotton; made in Iowa in 1989; machine pieced, hand quilted; traditional poly batt. $345.00

2020992 – BLUE COUNTRY WREATHS; 62" x 104"; assorted blue scraps w/white background & rosy pink bow on wreaths, blue paisley border & country blue backing w/tiny blue flowers; cotton; made in California in 1992; machine pieced, hand quilted; poly batting. $518.00

3020992 – UNKNOWN; 96" x 96"; dark avocado green, off-white, medium avocado & light brick red; made in Florida in 1992; 100% cotton; machine pieced, hand quilted; Mountain Mist lite batt; a reproduction of antique quilt – unusual in pointed & not straight edges. $862.00

4020992 – 9-PATCH; 64" x 80"; scraps w/green sashing; cotton; unknown maker – probably made in 1930's in Georgia; hand pieced & quilted; flour sack fabrics, gold print for back & binding; heavy cotton batting; one small mend & minor fading at edges. $230.00

5020992 – RED ROSE; 77" x 96"; red & white; cotton/polyester; made in Missouri in 1991; machine pieced & quilted; polyester batting. $172.00

6020992 – FLORAL HEIRLOOM; 83" x 106"; cream background, mauve, two values of rose, forest green, coordinating green & beige prints, mauve binding; 100% cotton; made in Ohio in 1992; applique patterns are detail of flowers, stems, leaves; border sprays of floral applique; emphasis on hand quilting! $535.00

7020992 – GRANDMOTHER'S FLOWER GARDEN; 78" x 90"; multicolored top, the path is black & rose flowered; cotton & cotton blends; made in Arkansas in 1990; hand pieced & quilted; low-loft batting; backing is washed muslin. $230.00

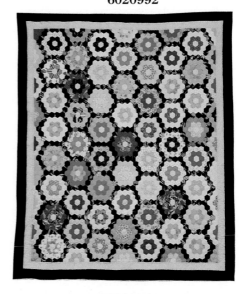

7020992

61

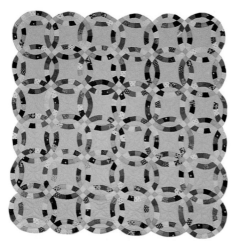

1030992

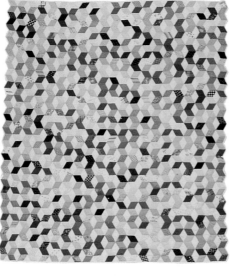

2030992

3030992

4030992

5030992

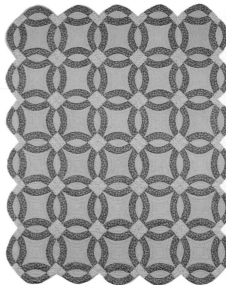

6030992

7030992

1030992 – DOUBLE WEDDING RING; 82" x 82"; light blue background w/multicolored rings; cotton; made in 1987 in Maryland; machine pieced, hand quilted; quilted seam by seam, Mountain Mist batting. $288.00

2030992 – TUMBLING BLOCKS; 78" x 87"; white background, a variety of solid colors & prints; cotton & cotton/poly blends; made in Arkansas in 1992; hand pieced & quilted; double bias binding. $259.00

3030992 – LOG CABIN STAR; 86" x 102"; navy blue w/rose & green on off-white background; cotton; made in Kansas in 1990; machine pieced, hand quilted; double binding, mitered corners, polyester batting. $345.00

4030992 – TREE OF LIFE; 88" x 90"; white background, blue, yellow, reds, country blues, green leaves, blue binding; cotton prints; made in Indiana in 1991; hand quilted, appliqued & embroidered; polyester batting, a Posey County Fair Indiana winner. $1,150.00

5030992 – PATCHWORK BLOCKS; 64" x 75"; multicolored fabrics possibly from the 1930's (bought at garage sale); cotton, satine, silk, brocade, etc; machine quilted in 1988 in Kentucky; polyester batting. $172.00

6030992 – DOUBLE WEDDING RING; 97" x 118"; rose, wine, light corners, beige background; cotton/polyester blend fabrics; made in Illinois in 1992; machine pieced, hand quilted; polyester batting, a king size traditional pattern. $247.00

7030992 – BRIDAL WREATH; 88" x 104"; off-white background w/earth tone colors green, brown & rust; all cotton top, cotton/poly backing; made in Kansas in 1991; hand quilted & appliqued; Hobbs polyester batting. $345.00

1040992

2040992

3040992

4040992

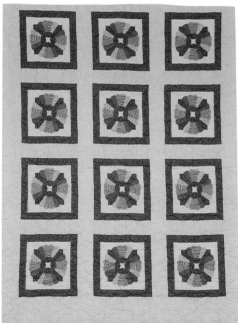

5040992↗

6040992

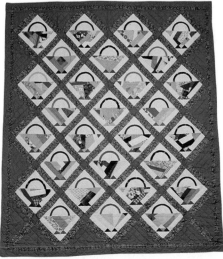

7040992

1040992 – FAN-TASTIC FLOWER OF AUTUMN; 34" x 34"; mauves & blues with a touch of silver; 100% prewashed cottons; made in New York in 1989; machine pieced, hand quilted; an unusual fan pattern set around a center star, low-loft polyester batting. $230.00

2040992 – JACOB'S LADDER; 90" x 96"; green; cotton & cotton/poly blend; made in Nebraska in 1990; handmade; polyester batting; in-the-ditch quilting w/bottom border. $460.00

3040992 – BEAR'S PAW; 53" x 53"; tea-dye background w/variety of prints for bear's paw; 100% cotton, prewashed; made in Louisiana in 1992; machine pieced, machine quilted in 1" diagonal lines; 100% cotton batt, washed for "antique look," double binding. $345.00

4040992 – ATTIC WINDOWS; 32" x 38"; lavender, teal blue, navy w/jungle print window scenes; all cotton; made in South Carolina in 1991; machine pieced, hand quilted, matching color threads; poly low-loft batting; original quilting design on borders of jungle animals & leaves; lavender backing, jungle print binding, in-the-ditch quilting around windows. $155.00

5040992 – DRESDEN PLATE; 72" x 88"; blue, mauve & off-white, lining off-white; cotton & cotton/polyester blends; made in Missouri in 1990; machine pieced & quilted using preprinted blocks; setting strips & border contain tiny blue flowers; machine quilted w/leaf design; poly batting. (Partial quilt shown in photo.)$144.00

6040992 – PLAIN PEACH; 44" x 55"; solid peach, beige print back; cotton/polyester fabrics; made in Illinois in 1990; hand quilted; baby size; reversible, poly batting. $55.00

7040992 – SCRAP BASKET; 87" x 98"; off-white, paisley print, country blue to set off basket design; cotton/poly blends; made in Oregon in 1991; machine pieced, hand quilted; Dacron™ batting; quilt was part of two folk-art exhibits in Portland, OR colleges. $345.00

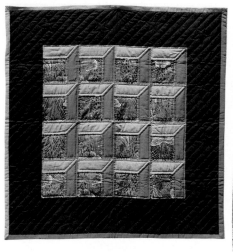

1050992

2050992

3050992

4050992

5050992

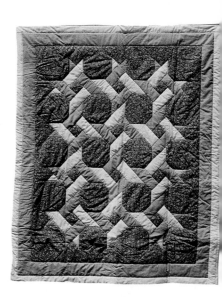

6050992

7050992

1050992 – NIGHT FLIGHT; 36" x 36"; black, green & pumpkin; 100% cotton; made in North Carolina in 1992; machine pieced, hand quilted; ¼" quilting, border diagonal quilting w/stars in design, two-color binding, 4" hanging sleeve. $70.00

2050992 – STAR IN HEAVEN; 92" x 105"; red, white & navy blue prints on white background; all cotton; made in Michigan in 1992; machine pieced, hand quilted; Mountain Mist polyester batting. $414.00

3050992 – CHRISTMAS SUNBONNET; 48" x 48"; red, green & ecru; cotton/polyester blends & cotton; made in Minnesota in 1990; hand pieced, quilted & appliqued; polyester batting, adapted from a pattern in *Quilter's Newsletter* Magazine, heavily quilted. $218.00

4050992 – BOX TURTLE; 45" x 68"; dark green, off-white & multicolored blocks; cotton; made in Kentucky in 1988; hand pieced & quilted; polyester batting; tumbling blocks on border, decorative designs of turtle-type reptiles. $575.00

5050992 – WINTERWONDERLAND WINDOWS; 45" x 33"; Christmas reds & greens, multicolored winter scene; 100% cotton; made in Washington in 1991; machine pieced & quilted; low-loft polyester batting; hanging sleeve; woodland creatures in a snowy field are seen through a picture window. $104.00

6050992 – AROUND THE TWIST; 42" x 50"; green, brown & tan; cotton; made in Idaho in 1992; machine pieced & quilted; Fairfield polyester batting. $70.00

7050992 – IRISH CHAIN; 84" x 102"; medium blue, black, off-white background; 100% cottons; hand quilted in 1992 in Nebraska, the maker and age of top is unknown, the top is hand & machined pieced; Mountain Mist polyester batting; antique quilt top newly quilted. $402.00

1060992

2060992

3060992

4060992

5060992

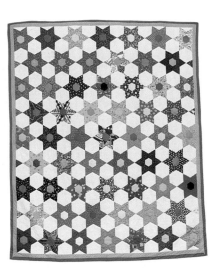

6060992

1060992 – GRANDMOTHER'S DIAMOND FIELD; 102" x 108"; color coordinated blocks set together with white, white lining, red binding; cotton; made in Alabama in 1988; hand pieced & quilted; polyester batting, quilted on each side of seam. $575.00

2060992 – TEDDY CRIB QUILT; 36" x 46"; yellow & white, brown bear, multicolored balloons; cotton/poly fabric; made in Illinois in 1991; crib quilt or wallhanging. $75.00

3060992 – AROUND THE WORLD; 88" x 92"; shades of mauve & old rose; cotton; made in Oklahoma in 1988; machine pieced, hand quilted in 1½" strips; polyfill poly batting. $632.00

4060992 – 4 POINT STAR VARIATION; 98" x 100"; multicolored stars on white background w/printed blue border; all cotton; quilted in Iowa in 1989; machine pieced, hand quilted; old top–newly quilted. $316.00

5060992 – LOG CABIN; 75" x 102"; light blue to dark blue w/white; cotton/poly blend fabrics; made in Illinois in 1991; machine pieced, hand quilted; polyester batting. $288.00

6060992 – SIX POINT STAR; 71" x 91"; multicolored print stars w/solid centers, two shades of green border, muslin background & backing, prints are in blues, browns, reds & greens, should go with anything; cotton/polyester blends; made in Ohio in 1989; hand pieced & quilted; polyester batting. $489.00

7060992 – AUNT ELIZIES STAR; 92" x 102"; red & white cotton scraps; made in Oregon in 1992; machine pieced & quilted; Mountain Mist Fatt Batt. $460.00

7060992

65

1070992

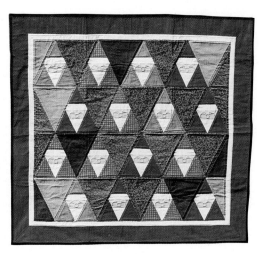

2070992

3070992

4070992

5070992

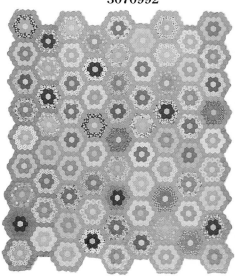

6070992

7070992

1070992 – BARNSTORM/GRANDMOTHER'S FAN/9 PATCH; these three wallhangings are to be sold as a unit; sizes 19" x 22", 14" x 18" & 15" x 15"; old red, navy & blue; blues; navy, off-white; machine pieced & quilted; polyfill batt; all three have sleeves for hanging. $126.00

2070992 – SANTA IN THE TREES; 41" x 38"; reds, greens & off-white, black bias binding mitered at corners; 100% cotton; made in Minnesota in 1991; machine pieced & quilted; Santa's eyes, nose & chubby cheeks are quilted into the triangles that make his face & beard. $86.00

3070992 – WHITE WEDDING RING; 60" x 90"; multicolored solids on unbleached muslin background; cotton, satins, cotton/poly blends; made in Virginia in 1991; machine pieced, hand quilted; quilting designs in open areas are feathered wreaths, hearts & variations, Mountain Mist polyester batting; double binding. $391.00

4070992 – 54-40 OR FIGHT; 84" x 98"; blue & white; cotton; made in Pennsylvania in 1990; machine pieced, hand quilted. $431.00

5070992 – SUNSET HOUSES; 39" x 52"; black houses, multicolored background & backing; 100% cotton; made in Indiana in 1991; machine pieced, hand quilted; polyester batting; black schoolhouses against a streaked sunset. $75.00

6070992 – FLOWER GARDEN; 72" x 84"; blues, violets w/green "path," backing is also green; made in Missouri Ozarks in 1930's; all hand made w/small stitches; thin batting, scalloped edges. $454.00

7070992 – BANBURY CROSS; 58" x 58"; black, red & green; 100% cotton; made in Wisconsin in 1991; machine pieced & quilted; polyester batting; colors are shaded to provide a central design focus. $98.00

66

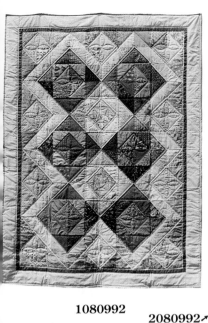

1080992

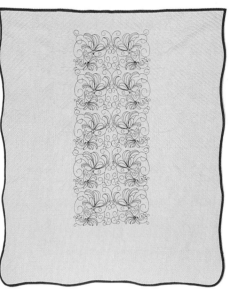

2080992 ↗

3080992

4080992

5080992

6080992

1080992 – 6 IN SHADE; 50" x 67"; variety of prints, warm tone, inner border brown, outer border yellow; cotton & cotton/poly blends, light print cotton backing; made in Illinois in 1992; machine pieced, hand quilted; poly batt; print fabrics, separated by lights & darks into a design framing 6 squares set on point. $259.00

2080992 – FLOWER BASKET; 84" x 102"; beige w/rose sashing, navy baskets w/rose & rose/navy print flowers; cotton/poly blends; made in Illinois in 1990; machine pieced, hand quilted; bonded polyester non-allergenic batting. (Border not completely shown.) $374.00

3080992 – FRIENDSHIP DAHLIA; 65" x 90"; yellow, white & multicolored calico prints; 100% prewashed cotton; made in Illinois in 1988; machine pieced, hand appliqued & quilted; yellow is quilted in spider web pattern; flower patterned back; Mountain Mist batting. $172.00

4080992 – OH! TANNENBAUM!; 37" x 41"; tiny Christmas prints, reds, greens, white printed background, solid white back; 100% cottons; made in Florida in 1985; machine pieced, hand quilted; poly batt; Log Cabin Tree has surprises (cross in center, appliqued candles w/ quilted halos, quilted holly); detailed quilting 1" apart on 1" strips. $138.00

5080992 – UNKNOWN; 84" x 96"; med. green embroidered on white; cotton; unknown maker; made in 1980's in Ohio; hand quilted & embroidered; poly batt; bound w/green bias binding. $259.00

6080992 – 9 PATCH & HEARTS; 42" x 46"; yellow, green, rust & white; 100% cotton; made in Wisconsin in 1989; machine pieced, hand quilted; Mountain Mist polyester batting. $172.00

7080992 – INDIAN HATCHET QUILT; 75" x 86"; yellow, orange & brown w/beige background & lining; cotton & cotton/poly blends; made in Ohio in 1990; hand pieced & quilted; Mountain Mist polyester batting. $374.00

7080992

1090992

2090992

3090992

4090992

5090992

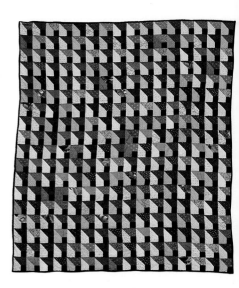

6090992

7090992

1090992 – 9 PATCH; 45" x 45"; purples, blues, burgundies, rose, dark green; cotton w/polyester; made by Amish group in Pennsylvania in 1986; machine pieced, hand quilted, excellent hand quilting. $172.00

2090992 – ENIGMA STAR; 82" x 95"; various shades of blue w/gray centers on white background set together w/light blue; cotton; made in Illinois in 1990; machine pieced, hand quilted; polyester batting. $288.00

3090992 – LOG CABIN; 40" x 40"; blues & various prints; cottons & blends; made in North Carolina in 1986; machine pieced, hand quilted; polyester batting. $150.00

4090992 – NO TITLE; 77" x 94"; white top w/lavender, rose pattern on back; cotton/polyester blend fabric; made in Pennsylvania in 1980; hand quilted; Dacron™ polyester batting. $345.00

5090992 – RISING STAR; 41" x 50"; black print, pink print, gray background; 100% cotton; made in Iowa in 1992; machine pieced, machine quilted in the ditch, hand quilted in borders, tied w/blue yarn; low-loft polyester batting; double bias binding; pink print back. $144.00

6090992 – ATTIC WINDOWS; 76" x 86"; many shades of prints & solids; 100% cotton; made in Wisconsin in 1991; machine pieced & quilted; extra-loft batting. $374.00

7090992 – LONE STAR; 90" x 96"; red, white & blue; cotton/polyester; made in Missouri in 1991; machine pieced & quilted; polyester batting. $230.00

1100992

2100992

3100992

4100992

5100992

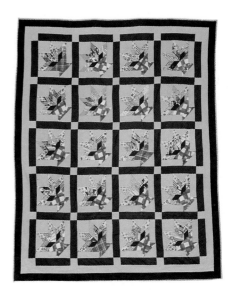

6100992

1100992 – EVENING STAR; 39" x 47"; blues, greens & off-white, 100% cotton; made in Georgia in 1992; machine pieced, hand quilted; polyester batting; has hanging sleeve. $115.00

2100992 – NINE PATCH; 74" x 96"; peach & off-white; 100% cotton calico & bleached muslin top; made in 1992 in South Carolina; machine pieced, hand quilted (outline & motif designs); lining of doublewide cloth (no seams), reversible to off-white except for peach double binding. $690.00

3100992 – TULIP; 32" x 32"; rose on off-white; cotton; made in Illinois in 1990; tablepiece or wallhanging. $126.00

4100992 – BETTY BOOP; 63" x 86"; light beige sashed w/peach color; 50/50 cotton/poly blend; made in Kentucky in 1991; machine pieced & quilted, hand painted; polyester batting, all-purpose quilt. $230.00

5100992 – ENCIRCLED TULIP; 94" x 102"; navy & light blue w/pink & white; all cotton fabrics; made in Kansas in 1992; machine pieced, hand appliqued & quilted; polyester batting; double binding, poly/cotton backing, mitered corners. $391.00

6100992 – BASKETS; 69" x 87"; yellow & green stripping; 100% cotton; baskets pieced in 1940, set in yellow dyed flour sack fabric, machine quilted in the ditch around squares, hand quilted inside squares, finished in 1986 in Alabama; yellow print on back; Hobbs polyester batting. $230.00

7100992 – HONEY BEE; 88" x 105"; shades of brown w/aqua, cream background; all cotton; made in Kansas in 1980; machine pieced, hand quilted & appliqued; poly/cotton backing, polyester batting, mitered corners; star quilted in squares, chain quilted in sashings. $299.00

7100992

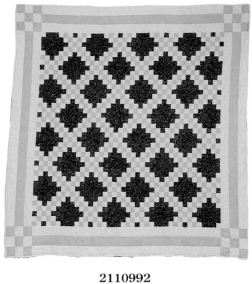

2110992

3110992

4110992

5110992

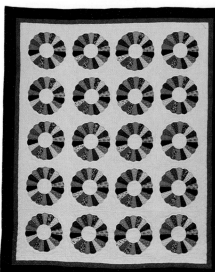

6110992

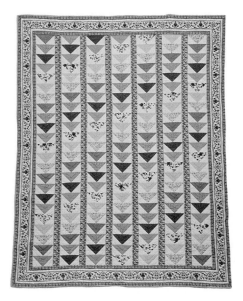

7110992

1110992 – SAMPLER; 58" x 90"; rainbow of colors; cotton & percale sheets 50/50; made in Massachusetts in 1988; hand pieced & quilted; polydown batting, reversible. $569.00

2110992 – DOUBLE IRISH CHAIN; 102" x 104"; brown & orange autumn leaves, beige chains, highlighted w/gold; 100% cotton, unbleached muslin lining (perma press); made in Hawaii in 1992; machine pieced & quilted; 9 patch corners; double fold binding; polyester batting; 4" borders quilted. $359.00

3110992 – PLAYFUL PUPPIES TRAIL; 66" x 88"; med. blue & blue checked w/multicolored puppies, black paws; sunshine yellow lining; prewashed cotton & cotton/poly blend fabrics; made in Kentucky in 1992; machine pieced & appliqued, hand quilted & embroidered; poly batt. $288.00

4110992 – CHRISTMAS TREE WALL QUILT; 41" x 41"; red, white, green Christmas prints; 100% cotton; made in Illinois in 1992; machine pieced, hand quilted at 1" & 1½" intervals w/red thread; Quilt lite batting; printed backing w/rod pocket for hanging. $172.00

5110992 – TEXAS PINE TREE EVERLASTING; 87" x 100"; red, gold; cotton/polyester prewashed; made in Texas in 1990; machine pieced, hand quilted; hand embroidered Texas stars & pine cones on border areas; Mountain Mist medium thickness poly batting. $420.00

6110992 – DRESDEN PLATE; 79" x 83"; browns & beiges; cotton & cotton/polyester blends; made in California in 1991; hand appliqued & quilted; brown & beige "plates" on the white background, polyester batting, lots of quilting. $385.00

7110992 – FLYING GEESE; 71" x 87"; blues, slate tan, cream; cotton; made in Nebraska in 1992; machine pieced, hand quilted; polyfill batting; light blue backing. $385.00

70

1120992

2120992

3120992

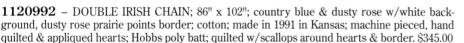

4120992

5120992

6120992

1120992 – DOUBLE IRISH CHAIN; 86" x 102"; country blue & dusty rose w/white background, dusty rose prairie points border; cotton; made in 1991 in Kansas; machine pieced, hand quilted & appliqued hearts; Hobbs poly batt; quilted w/scallops around hearts & border. $345.00

2120992 – 8 POINT STAR VARIATION; 92" x 108"; lavender & navy, blue on white background; 100% cotton; made in Iowa in 1991; machine sewn top, hand quilted; traditional Mountain Mist batt, lavender in sets & border. $316.00

3120992 – DRESDEN PLATE; 85" x 102"; blue & rose, multicolored plate, white background; cotton w/cotton/poly back; made in Kansas in 1991; machine pieced, hand appliqued & quilted; 100% poly batt; hearts quilted in sashing w/a rose quilted in corner blocks; mitered corners & double bias binding. $345.00

4120992 – SNOW COUNTRY; 96" x 100"; yellow, pink, orange, blue & green; 100% cotton; made in Idaho in 1991; hand quilted, machine pieced; Fairfield extra loft batt. $460.00

5120992 – TRIPLE IRISH CHAIN; 85" x 103"; country blue, mauve, light blue & white; cotton & cotton/poly blends; made in Indiana in 1992; machine pieced & quilted; poly batt; appliqued mauve hearts on a white square, corner 9-patches; dark & med. fabrics are used to frame the quilt. $213.00

6120992 – LOG CABIN; 78" x 94"; pink & black, solids & small prints; cotton & cotton/poly blends; made in Georgia in 1992; machine pieced, hand quilted; Mountain Mist poly batt; borders pieced in a way to give a different look. $454.00

7120992 – STAR & HEARTS; 88" x 102"; shades of navy & mauve; all cotton w/polyester batt; made in Kansas in 1991; machine pieced, hand quilted & appliqued; double binding, mitered corners. $345.00

7120992

1130992

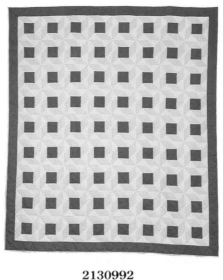

2130992

3130992

4130992

5130992

6130992

7130992

1130992 – TRIP AROUND THE WORLD; 73" x 86"; multicolored, older fabrics; cotton & cotton/poly blends; made in Alabama in 1989; hand pieced & quilted; poly batt. $230.00

2130992 – LITTLE BOX; 80" x 89"; country blue & light pink, white backing; made in Arkansas in 1990; machine pieced, hand quilted; hearts in border & squares; poly batt; double bias binding; white broadcloth backing & binding. $230.00

3130992 – IRISH CHAIN W/FOLK HEARTS; 80" x 102"; predominantly rose w/gray & white, quilt backing matches rose pindot background; 100% cotton; made in Connecticut in 1991; machine pieced, hand quilted w/folk art design quilted around hearts & swag w/tulip design quilted in border area. $460.00

4130992 – AMISH STARS; 68" x 103"; purple, bright blue, yellow, green, red, black background; 100% cotton; made in Delaware in 1992; machine pieced, hand quilted w/soft gray thread; Hobbs dark-colored batt; 8 star blocks in Amish colors, purple & green sashing, borders black, plum-colored backing & bias binding. $374.00

5130992 – ATTIC WINDOWS "SHADOW'S DREAM"; 34" x 41"; purple, lavender, black w/yellow, blue & jade; cotton; made in Virginia in 1991; machine pieced, hand quilted; poly batt; featuring tropical birds, plants & butterflies. $201.00

6130992 – AMISH; 34" x 34"; black & mauve; cotton blends; made in Nebraska in 1992; machine pieced, hand quilted; polyfill batt; feather quilting in center. $101.00

7130992 – OHIO ROSE VARIATION; 101" x 101"; light & med. peach, rose & green; cotton & some cotton/poly blends on solids; made in Washington in 1991; machine pieced, hand quilted & appliqued. $575.00

1140992

2140992

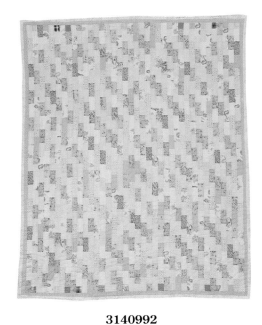

3140992

4140992

5140992

6140992

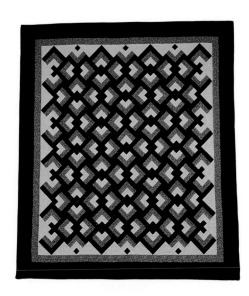

7140992

1140992 – PLAIN REVERSIBLE; 42" x 61"; solid white on one side, print on the other (side shown); cotton/poly; hand quilted baby quilt; made in Illinois in 1990; Dacron™ batt. $60.00

2140992 – GRANDMOTHER'S FAN; 30" x 29"; mauves, greens, black, tan & cream; 100% cotton, embellishments of lace, pearls; made in Indiana in 1990; hand & machine pieced, hand quilted; Fairfield polyester batting. $110.00

3140992 – BRICKWORK; 79" x 93"; assorted pastels & prints, lining is light pink, blue floral; cotton & cotton/poly blend fabrics; made in Virginia in 1988; machine pieced, hand quilted; Polyfill traditional batting, quilted in fan pattern. $316.00

4140992 – CORN WOMEN; 48" x 64"; light brown backing, strips of various colors & animals; cotton; made in Kentucky in 1988; hand pieced & quilted; polyester batting; Native American pattern of corn woman, Seminole Indian strip & strips of various animals & birds. $575.00

5140992 – SEASON'S GREETINGS; 43" x 43"; Christmas side consists of blues, yellows, black; reverse side has greens, browns, rusts, pumpkin, gold & black; 100% cotton; made in Iowa in 1991; machine appliqued & quilted; reversible wallhanging–one side for Christmas, the other for autumn (side shown); all fabrics except black hand dyed. $345.00

6140992 – BIRD OF PARADISE; 78" x 94"; green & white; cotton top, cotton/polyester blend backing; made in Ohio in 1991; hand quilted & appliqued; poly batt; old pattern, new quilt. $518.00

7140992 – LOVER'S KNOT; 98" x 110"; mauve going to light purple, dark purple, black w/mauves etched w/gold; 100% cotton; made in Minnesota in 1991; machine pieced, hand quilted; polyester batting. $518.00

73

1150992

2150992

3150992

4150992

5150992

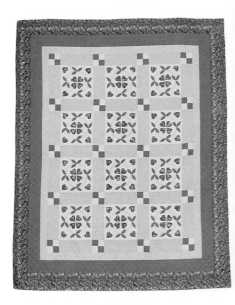

6150992

7150992

1150992 – WINDMILL; 70" x 88"; blue & green; cotton & cotton/polyester fabrics; made in Illinois in 1990; machine pieced, hand quilted; blue pindots & green floral calico; Mountain Mist batting; quilted on both sides of seam. $126.00

2150992 – GRANDMOTHER'S FANCY FAN; 76" x 106"; white background, pastel fans w/black trim & centers, pastel; cotton & cotton/polyester; made in Illinois in 1990; machine pieced, hand quilted; ultra-loft lightweight polyester batt; pastel fabrics. $690.00

3150992 – BLUE SKIES; 84" x 104"; blues, light blue back; cottons; made in Pennsylvania in 1992; machine pieced, hand quilted; polyester batting; double binding; may be reversed. $402.00

4150992 – SCRAP CHECKERBOARD; 28" x 31"; multicolored scraps & muslin; cotton; made in North Carolina in 1992; machine pieced & quilted; diagonal quilting on muslin, cotton classic batting, pieced scrap border. $115.00

5150992 – TRIANGLE COMBINATION SAMPLER; 40" x 40"; brown, peach, blue calico; 100% cotton; made in Montana in 1990; machine pieced & quilted; polyester batting. $60.00

6150992 – PENNSYLVANIA DUTCH PRINT; 74" x 93"; brown, rust, unbleached muslin; 100% cotton; made in Alabama in 1988; machine pieced & quilted; squares set w/muslin background & brown stripping; design of blocks repeated in border by machine quilting; Hobbs poly batt. $230.00

7150992 – ENCIRCLED TULIP; 96" x 109"; different shades of rose, off-white backing; 100% cotton prints, 50/50 background; made in Missouri in 1990; machine pieced, hand quilted; poly batt. $402.00

74

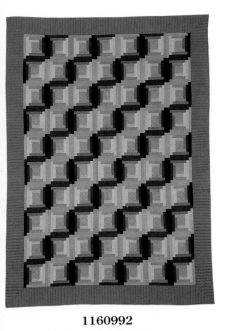

1160992

2160992

3160992

4160992

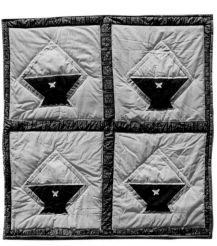

5160992

6160992

7160992

1160992 – LOG CABIN; 74" x 99"; muted blues, pink, gray, lavender, aqua & black w/dusty blue back; solid cotton fabrics; made in Illinois in 1991; machine pieced, hand quilted. $569.00

2160992 – PINEAPPLE; 31" x 31"; purple, light green, pink; 100% cotton prints & hand-painted cotton; made in Pennsylvania in 1991; machine pieced, machine quilted w/metallic thread. $86.00

3160992 – CARPENTER'S WHEEL; 88" x 103"; blue, red w/off-white background; 100% cotton; made in Tennessee in 1990; hand pieced & quilted w/feather design; Mountain Mist batting. $1,438.00

4160992 – BEAR'S PAW; 84" x 104"; white-on-white muslin, cranberry rose, dark green; 100% cotton; made in North Carolina in 1992; machine pieced, free-motion machine quilted; polyester batting, traditional pattern in modern decorator colors. $402.00

5160992 – BASKETS OF FLOWERS; 47" x 47"; light blue, navy, flowers are light pink, off-white back, lace on handles & down basket; cotton; made in Wisconsin in 1992; machine pieced & quilted; poly batt; pink satin ribbon across middle of basket & white crocheted butter-fly on bottom. $115.00

6160992 – SHIPS AT SEA SCRAP QUILT; 88" x 102"; white, light & dark blue, scrap cali-coes, touch of red; cotton/poly blend fabric; made in Illinois in 1991; hand quilted; poly batt. $345.00

7160992 – TRIP AROUND THE WORLD; 89" x 96"; soft greens, violet, calicoes, red prints–all colors; cotton; made in Nebraska in 1930's, maker unknown; all handmade w/tiny stitches, thin batting, white muslin backing, soft green border w/hearts. $489.00

75

1170992

2170992

3170992

4170992

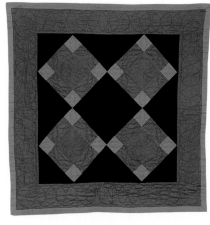

5170992

6170992

7170992

1170992 – HEXAGONS; 65" x 79"; green background, multicolored hexagons; cotton/poly blends; unknown maker, top age unknown; hand pieced; hand quilted; made in Kentucky in 1991; poly batt. $196.00

2170992 – BEIGE REVERSIBLE; 45" x 60"; unbleached muslin, yellow print back (shown); hand quilted; made in Illinois in 1990; Dacron™ batting. $60.00

3170992 – SPRING FLOWERS (APPLIQUED); 74" x 88"; light green w/darker green leaves & stems, white & yellow flowers, white border & white scalloped edging; cotton; made in early 1900's in Western Wisconsin – maker unknown; hand quilted; yellow & white daffodils w/darker green stems & leaves in the middle – bunches of same flowers & buds in corners; scalloped border; feathers quilted in border, under & around center medallion. $345.00

4170992 – GRAPE BASKET; 83" x 95"; dark pink & white; cotton; made in Texas in 1992; machine pieced, hand quilted; Mountain Mist polyester batting; feather wreath quilting in plain blocks. $345.00

5170992 – PUSS IN THE CORNER; 22" x 22"; traditional Amish colors–turquoise, purple, turkey red & black; 100% cotton, cotton flannel batt; made in Michigan in 1985; heavily quilted w/black quilting thread – intertwined circles, flowers, leaves & cross hatch; hanging tabs. $80.00

6170992 – TURNING TRIANGLES; 80" x 90"; white background w/various colors; cotton & polyester/cotton blends; made in Arkansas in 1991; hand pieced & quilted; assorted prints & solids; double bias binding. $230.00

7170992 – LOG CABIN; 99" x 119"; red & beige, beige backing; polyester/cotton blend fabrics; made in Illinois in 1991; machine pieced; Dacron™ poly Super Fluff batt. $230.00

1180992

2180992

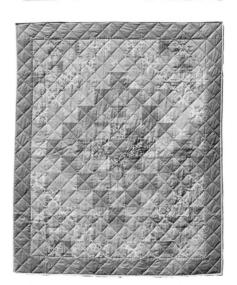

3180992 ↗

4180992

5180992

6180992

1180992 – FOUR BASKETS; 88" x 108"; colonial blue, mauve & off-white; perma press cotton/poly blend fabric; made in Missouri in 1992; machine pieced, hand quilted; quilted seam by seam, embroidered basket handles; off-white backing. $345.00

2180992 – STAR TRIAS; 34" x 34"; pinks, blues & greens, off-white background; 100% cotton; made in Idaho in 1992; machine pieced, hand quilted; Mountain Mist batting; stars are fabric scraps. $126.00

3180992 – MAPLE LEAF; 78" x 108"; red & white; mercerized broadcloth; made in Virginia in 1990; hand pieced (double sewed), hand quilted; polyfill batting; this quilt long enough to cover pillows. $288.00

4180992 – RISING STAR LOG CABIN; 82" x 105"; peaches, moted apricot, tans, browns (all calico prints), solid peach backing; 100% cotton; made in Virginia in 1992; machine pieced, hand quilted; pieced w/narrow strips quilted 1¼" apart through centers, quilting shows on both sides; double bias binding matches quilt, mitered corners, polyester batting. $575.00

5180992 – PASSION SUN; 45" x 45"; pinks & cream; broadcloth & muslin; made in South Carolina in 1989; machine pieced, hand quilted; gentle sun surrounded by 4 stars, lot of quilting throughout. $230.00

6180992 – TRIP AROUND THE WORLD; 44" x 51"; blue, white & pastel pink solids & prints; 100% cotton chintz & polished cottons; made in Georgia in 1992; machine pieced, hand quilted; backing is blue/pink print, binding is pink; quilted w/white thread. $184.00

7180992 – STAR; 91" x 111"; mauve w/cream fill; cotton/polyester fabric; made in Missouri in 1991; machine pieced & quilted; polyester batting. $230.00

7180992

1190992

2190992

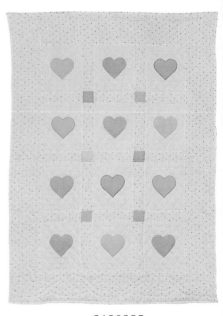

3190992

4190992

5190992

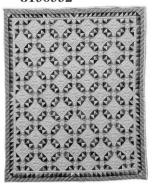

6190992

7190992

1190992 – A VICTORIAN BRIDE'S STYLE; 90" x 108"; pink & off-white; lightly glazed (65 poly/35 cotton) chintz & long-fiber 100% cotton muslin; made in Utah in 1991; hand quilted w/cotton-wrapped poly quilting thread; double bias bound in chintz of darker pink, Dacron™ batt. $850.00

2190992 – LOVE RING VARIATION; 83" x 100"; blue w/cream backing; cotton/poly blends; made in Missouri in 1991; machine pieced & quilted; poly batt. $230.00

3190992 – HEARTS CRIB QUILT; 36" x 50"; multicolored tiny hearts print appliqued on white background; cotton/poly blend fabric; made in Illinois in 1991; machine appliqued, hand quilted. $86.00

4190992 – BASKET; 43" x 56"; cream background w/rose & green, cabbage roses, rose; 100% cottons; made in Colorado in 1992; machine pieced, hand quilted & appliqued; poly batt; basket blocks circled by double sawtooth border; quilting has lots of hearts; double bias binding. $230.00

5190992 – FLORAL PATTERN; 76" x 92"; multicolored flowers on white background; cotton; made in Illinois in 1981; hand appliqued, embroidered & quilted; poly batt; quilting in intricate patterns. $402.00

6190992 – DAISY CHAIN; 80" x 95"; predominately pink, multicolored triangles on off-white background on white backing; all cotton; made in Maryland in 1988; machine pieced, hand quilted; polyfill batt, has hanging sleeve, never used. $431.00

7190992 – BASKET; 82" x 104"; blue, pink & white; cotton; made in Kentucky in 1991; hand pieced & quilted; Mountain Mist poly batt; feather wreath quilting; material prewashed. $345.00

1011292

2011292

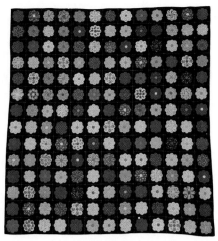

3011292

4011292

5011292

6011292

7011292

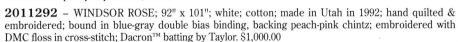

1011292 – FLORAL TRELLIS; 87" x 103"; beige, rose & blue; 100% cotton; made in North Carolina in 1992; machine pieced, free-motion machine quilted; polyester batting; quilting design enhances three-dimensional quality of pattern. $402.00

2011292 – WINDSOR ROSE; 92" x 101"; white; cotton; made in Utah in 1992; hand quilted & embroidered; bound in blue-gray double bias binding, backing peach-pink chintz; embroidered with DMC floss in cross-stitch; Dacron™ batting by Taylor. $1,000.00

3011292 – MIDNIGHT FLOWERS; 87" x 92"; black with gingham (all colors) flowers; cotton fabric; made in Kentucky in 1986; hand pieced & quilted, gingham flower pattern appliqued on 6½" square black blocks, with white briar stitch around each block. $402.00

4011292 – LOG CABIN IN BARN RAISING STYLE; 84" x 104"; dark green & white; cotton and cotton/polyester blends; made in Indiana in 1992; machine pieced & quilted; polyester batting; braided border in the border. $230.00

5011292 – AFRIKAANS; 60" x 80"; black background, navy border, appliqued figures in red, yellow, green, white, gold & brown, beige backing; 100% cotton top & backing; made in California in 1991; hand appliqued & quilted w/red quilt thread; figures & animals all hand appliqued in an African Dahomey style; very fine hand quilting; quilt was accepted into the 1992 AQS show; has hanging sleeve. $575.00

6011292 – DRUNKARD'S PATH; 76" x 88"; red & white; cotton broadcloth; made in Illinois in 1975; hand & machine pieced, hand quilted; Mountain Mist polyester batting; pieced border with shaped edges. $518.00

7011292 – LOVE RING; 84" x 84"; various shades of pink to rose with brown tone prints; cotton; made in Illinois in 1976; hand & machine pieced, hand quilted; Mountain Mist polyester batting. $460.00

1021292

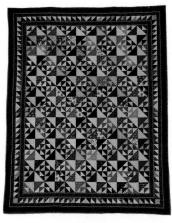

2021292

3021292

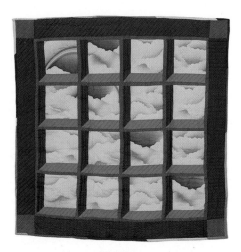

4021292

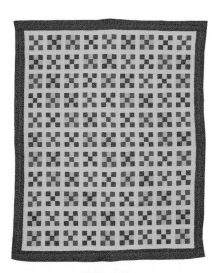

5021292

6021292

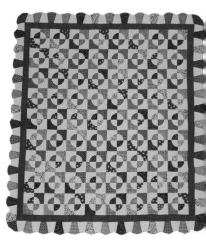

7021292

1021292 – WAKE-UP CALL; 104" x 110"; off-white background with multicolored high-quality prints; cotton & cotton/polyester blend fabrics; made in Utah in 1992; machine pieced, hand quilted, Dacron™ filling; back is chintz with a black background covered with multicolored, large floral print, bound with dark sage-green double bias binding; original design from Drunkard's Path block. $989.00

2021292 – COUNTRY COUSINS; 64" x 78"; mixed darks & lights, brown tone borders; mostly cotton with probably some cotton/polyester blend fabrics; made in Illinois in 1982; hand & machine pieced, hand quilted; Mountain Mist polyester batting. $575.00

3021292 – CRYSANTHEMUM; 81" x 81"; light peach background, coral to brown crysanthemum colors; cottons & blends; made in Illinois in 1982; hand & machine pieced, hand quilted in feather design; fancy border with shaped edges; Mountain Mist polyester batting; Home Art Studio pattern. $575.00

4021292 – LOOK FOR THE RAINBOW; 38" x 39"; printed sky fabric, greens & orange; 100% cotton; made in Maine in 1991; machine pieced, hand quilted; polyester batting; crib quilt or wallhanging. $167.00

5021292 – NINEPATCH; 41" x 50"; blue & yellow prints with pale yellow lattice; all cotton; made in Indiana in 1992; machine pieced, hand quilted; ninety-nine 3" blocks; 1" lattice; 2½" border with matching binding; densely quilted. $201.00

6021292 – BED OF ROSES; 84" x 102"; colonial greens, rose, pink & white; cotton; made in Pennsylvania in 1992. $448.00

7021292 – STEEPLE CHASE; 77" x 84"; multi-red prints on white; cottons; made in Illinois in 1976; hand & machine pieced, hand quilted; pieced shaped border. $460.00

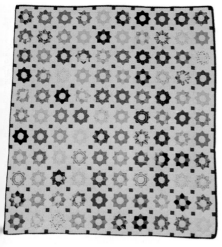

1031292

2031292

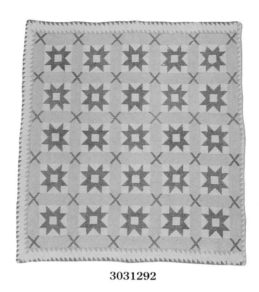

3031292

4031292

5031292

6031292

7031292

1031292 – STAR BOUQUET; 77" x 84"; white background with green squares, yellow centers; cotton & cotton/polyester blend fabrics; made in Arkansas in 1992; hand pieced & quilted; various prints & solids; double binding. $259.00

2031292 – LOG CABIN; 44" x 44"; pastel blues, pinks, lavenders with beige border; 100% cotton; made in Georgia in 1991; machine pieced, hand quilted; polyester batting; sleeve for hanging. $172.00

3031292 – VARIABLE STAR; 75" x 78"; green, white & pink; cotton; made in late 1800's by unknown maker in upstate New York; hand pieced & quilted; quilted with thin cotton batt; very good condition, but binding is slightly worn; some fading; print back has two very small stains & minor fading. $391.00

4031292 – FLOWER BLOSSOM; 87" x 98"; background white broadcloth, blue print, solid rose & white; broadcloth fabric; made in Arkansas in 1989; hand & machine pieced, hand quilted; polyester batting; double diamonds quilted in blue border. $230.00

5031292 – SPINNING ECHO; 35" x 35"; pink, yellow & green solids (no prints); 100% cotton; made in Illinois in 1987; machine pieced, hand quilted; soft colors in a contemporary pinwheel; polyester batting; hanging sleeve on back. $115.00

6031292 – TRIP AROUND THE WORLD; 78" x 90"; various blues & white; 50% cotton/polyester; made in Kentucky 1990; hand pieced, quilting by machine; polyester batting; hand pieced with light & dark materials to give a sunshine & shadow look. $201.00

7031292 – OWL WALL QUILT; 50" x 50"; fall colors; cotton; made in Arkansas in 1991; polyfil batting; hand pieced & quilted; owls have button eyes, hanging sleeve on back. $98.00

1041292

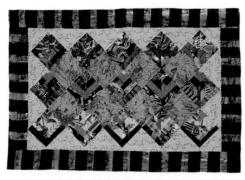

2041292

3041292

4041292

5041292

6041292

1041292 – COLONIAL LADIES; 66" x 72"; multicolors w/pink stripping; cotton; made in 1940's by unknown maker in Texas; ladies are hand appliqued & embroidered; set together by machine; hand quilted w/cotton batting; background is all quilted; some pencil quilting marks can be seen. $191.00

2041292 – JUNGLE PEEK-A-BOO; 35" x 24"; blue, green, orange & purple; 100% cotton; made in 1989 in Indiana; machine pieced, hand quilted; Hobbs black batting; border material printed in Africa; variety of "jungle" & "African" prints shelter lions & cubs that "peek out at you." $70.00

3041292 – RAIL FENCE; 36" x 52"; mauve, pink & white floral prints, pink floral backing; cotton; made in Oregon in 1992; machine pieced, hand tied; polyester batting. $40.00

4041292 – DOUBLE IRISH CHAIN; 79" x 95"; shamrock green & pure white; 100% cottons; made in Virginia in 1992; machine pieced, hand quilted, hand appliqued corners in blocks; low loft batting; reversible (all white back); heavily quilted; double bias bound. $575.00

5041292 – SCRAP QUILT BARN RAISING PATTERN; 90" x 105"; navy, hunter green & maroon w/assorted neutral lights, backed w/white/muslin floral print; 100% cotton; made in Connecticut in 1992; machine pieced, hand quilted; polyester low-loft batting, double bias binding; small quilting stitches. $448.00

6041292 – SUNFLOWER; 80" x 90"; white background, yellow flowers, gold print, orange/red/light brown flowered prints, brown & green stems & leaves; cotton prints; made in Indiana in 1989; hand pieced & quilted; polyester batting; won honors at county fair. $690.00

7041292 – STREAK OF LIGHTNING; 79" x 87"; light-medium assorted colors, lining is eggshell; cotton & cotton/polyester blends; made in Virginia in 1987; machine pieced, hand quilted; Polyfil traditional batting; all new materials, laundered once to remove markings; handmade double bias binding; quilted ½" around each block. $345.00

7041292

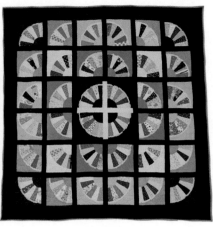

1051292

2051292

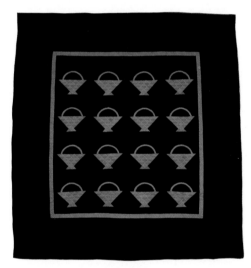

3051292

4051292

5051292

6051292

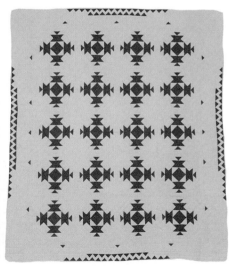

7051292

1051292 – FAN QUILT; 84" x 84"; blue, black, burgundy, rose & peach; cotton & cotton blends; made in Arkansas in 1991; machine pieced & quilted, lace trimmed fans; polyfil batt, cotton blend muslin backing; never used. $126.00

2051292 – TEXAS STAR; 88" x 88"; white background, pale yellows to gold to orange; cotton; unknown maker c.1940 (?); hand pieced star, machine pieced border, all hand quilted; muslin backing, no rips or tears, bright summer-type quilt. $914.00

3051292 – BASKET; 74" x 93"; pink & white; cotton; made in Kentucky in 1992; hand pieced & quilted; made of prewashed fabric, Mountain Mist batting. $316.00

4051292 – STREAK OF LIGHTNING; 48" x 50"; white, orange print, dark blue print, medium brown print; cotton; made in North Carolina in 1992; machine pieced & quilted; light, medium & dark values create strong diagonal design; wallhanging or crib quilt; thin polyester batting; dark blue binding & backing. $86.00

5051292 – SCRAP BASKETS; 40" x 40"; background in muslin, baskets in brown, multicolored; 100% cotton; made in North Carolina in 1991; machine pieced & quilted (diagonally every 2"); low loft batting. $60.00

6051292 – BASKETS; 112" x 112"; black with baskets of salmon pink & green; black backing; cotton; made in Colorado in 1990; hand quilted, hand & machine appliqued; black thread used with tiny stitches & extensive quilting with feather, cable & scroll design, never used. $575.00

7051292 – ANVIL CHORUS; 90" x 100"; deep red background in block, small medium blue flowers, green leaves, natural muslin backing (the red, blue & green print fabric shows up in photo as a reddish brown solid); perma press print & natural muslin; made in California in 1991; hand & machine pieced, hand quilted; Mountain Mist batting; shown San Diego Quilt Show. $460.00

83

3061292

1061292

2061292

6061292

4061292

5061292

1061292 – EMBROIDERED FLOWERS; 84" x 105"; white & blue; polyester/cotton blends; made in Missouri in 1991; machine pieced, hand quilted; polyester batting; hand embroidered with hand drawn, mostly original, flowers, original quilting pattern on border. $196.00

2061292 – ROSES; 74" x 92"; shades of pink & green on white; cotton; made in Illinois in 1974; hand appliqued & quilted; polyester batting, well quilted & pleasing to the eye. $575.00

3061292 – PINWHEELS; 82" x 82"; rainbow of bright colors; cotton and cotton/polyester blend fabrics; made in Kentucky in 1991; hand & machine pieced, machine quilted; polyester batting, reversible w/beautiful rainbow candy colors, could be used as a bedspread. $288.00

4061292 – TREE OF LIFE; 84" x 94"; white, country blue, blue, light blues, reds, yellows, brown stems and some green stems; cotton; made in Indiana in 1992; hand pieced, quilted, appliqued & embroidered; polyester batting, county fair ribbon winner. $1150.00

5061292 – TWINKLE, TWINKLE; 54" x 70"; a subtle cream print background sets off scrap stars; 100% prewashed cotton; made in Wisconsin in 1991; machine pieced & quilted; low loft polyester batting, traditional colors and design offer versatile decorating possibilities. $150.00

6061292 – TRIANGLE COMBINATION; 50" x 63"; blue & pink with yellow sets & borders; all cotton; made in Montana; machine quilted; polyester batting, four patch blocks of triangles in various arrangements. $50.00

7061292 – ROSE; 96" x 100"; background white, roses are several shades of pink & red, green leaves & stems; cotton; hand appliqued & hand quilted; quiltmaker worked on it for several years. $690.00

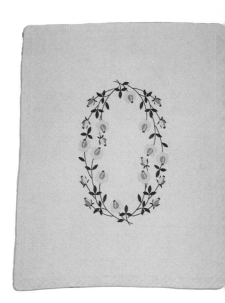

7061292

1071292

2071292

3071292

4071292

5071292

6071292

7071292

1071292 – LOG CABIN FAN; 88" x 102"; colors of different blues with white; all cotton with cotton/polyester backing; made in Kansas in 1991; machine pieced, hand quilted; mitered corners & double binding, a fan quilted in each fan block. $414.00

2071292 – SNAIL'S TRAIL; 90" x 100"; raspberry red with white background; 100% cotton; made in Missouri in 1990; machine pieced, hand quilted; Mountain Mist batting, one stain on border. $299.00

3071292 – COURTHOUSE STEPS; 83" x 102"; blues, mauves, beiges, brown; cotton; made in Ohio in 1992; machine pieced, hand quilted with various pattterns; polyester batting, neatly hand bound with double fabric. $454.00

4071292 – PASTEL GARDEN; 48" x 56"; beige background, pastel colors: beige, taupe, light browns, blue & rust; cottons & polished cottons; made in North Carolina in 1984; machine pieced, hand quilted; flannel batting, soft pastel colors, birds and blue & rust flowers on beige background. $230.00

5071292 – SCOTTY DOG; 36" x 52"; red & green tartan plaid with black puppies on white background, red plaid backing; blend fabrics; made in Oregon in 1992; machine pieced & appliqued, hand tied; polyester batting, baby quilt. $50.00

6071292 – LONE STAR; 95" x 109"; forest green; prints 100% cotton, the off-white is cotton/polyester blend (50/50); made in Missouri in 1992; machine pieced, hand quilted; polyester batting. $402.00

7071292 – BEARS PAW; 76" x 90"; off-white, blue & red; cotton/polyester blends; made in Illinois in 1992; hand quilted, machine pieced; polyester batting, pieced blocks of blue & red with off-white top & backing. $276.00

1081292

2081292

3081292

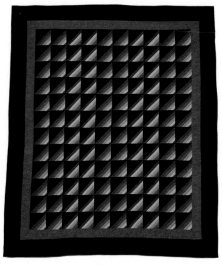

4081292

5081292

6081292

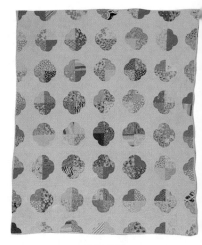

7081292

1081292 – BASKET; 44" x 56"; rose, pink & white; 100% cottons; made in Colorado in 1991; machine pieced, hand quilted & appliqued; cotton classic batt, heavily quilted, double bias binding, sleeve for hanging. $230.00

2081292 – WILD GOOSE CHASE; 76" x 94"; navy & antique white; cotton; made in Texas in 1992; hand pieced & quilted; fine quilting, feather wreaths in plain blocks, outline quilting of triangles. $345.00

3081292 – LOG CABIN; 47" x 46"; lavender, pinks, beige; flowered and solids in cotton; made in Wisconsin in 1991; mostly hand quilted, borders machine stitched; polyester batting. $115.00

4081292 – AMISH SHADOWS; 92" x 103"; black with various shades of maroon; cotton; made in 1991 by Amish in Lancaster, PA; machine pieced, hand quilted; medium thick batting, hearts in one border, colored thread on black, maroon-colored backing and binding, tiny quilting stitches. $632.00

5081292 – SUNBONNET GIRLS; 80" x 100"; white background, green borders; made in 1986 in Pennsylvania; machine pieced, hand appliqued & quilted; cotton fabrics with polyester batting, double binding, never been used. $288.00

6081292 – DOUBLE DAHLIA; 83" x 104"; 2 values of solid rose, print of roses with small accents of wine & cream, harmonizing soft green, cream background, borders of rose, green & rose print, rose print binding; 100% cottons; made in Ohio in 1992; hand quilting with sculptured designs of flowers, bows & leaves; hand appliqued dahlias, stems & leaves; hand bound with double fabric. $518.00

7081292 – HEARTS & GIZZARDS; 62" x 75"; off-white background, multicolored hearts; 100% cotton; made in 1930's, maker unknown (Kansas); hand pieced & quilted, backing is machine pieced sugar & flour sacks brought to the front for binding; some of the sack printing is still legible on the beige background; some age spots, but excellent condition overall. $191.00

1091292

2091292

3091292

4091292

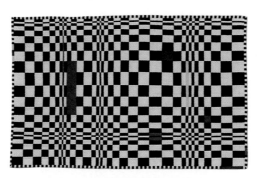

5091292

6091292

7091292

1091292 – TRIP AROUND THE WORLD; 78" x 96"; shades of purple, dusty rose & off-white; 100% cotton prints & cotton blend back; made in New York in 1987; machine pieced & quilted, hand tied; polyester batting. $126.00

2091292 – LUCKY ROSE; 90" x 102"; pink & mauve; whole cloth; made in 1992 in Oklahoma by Amish; hand quilted; "Lucky Horse" medallion quilted in the center. $230.00

3091292 – HUNTERS STAR; 20" x 36"; navy, light blue with dark pink border, all solid colors; cotton & cotton/polyester blends; made in Florida in 1992; machine pieced, hand quilted; polyester fleece batting, mitered corners; light blue backing with extended binding; has rod pocket. $75.00

4091292 – PLUMB PURPLE; 54" x 54"; purple shades, raspberry, avocado & gold on pale lavender background; cotton & cotton blends; made in Indiana in 1991; machine pieced, hand quilted & appliqued; 3-dimensional flowers with gold beads; back side embroidered with flowers, spiders & butterflies on print material; extra-loft poly batting; has rod pocket. $500.00

5091292 – OP–ART MONDRIAN; 46" x 28"; black, white, scattered brights; 100% cotton; made in Washington in 1992; machine pieced & quilted with silver metallic thread; cotton classic batting; has rod pocket. $115.00

6091292 – V.I.P. COLORWORKS QUILT; 39" x 39"; entire Colorworks Collection; V.I.P. 100% cotton Colorworks Fabrics; made in Illinois in 1992; machine pieced, hand quilted; has rod pocket; Mountain Mist light batting; won a 3rd place ribbon at the Heart of Illinois Fair in July, 1992. $242.00

7091292 – ENGLISH COUNTRY SAMPLER; 41" x 41"; soft greens, pinks, mauves, touches of wine & old gold, ecru print background; 100% prewashed cotton fabrics; made in 1991 in North Carolina; hand & machine pieced, hand appliqued & quilted; lowloft polyester batting, lots of hand quilting, designed as a teacher's sample. $172.00

1101292

2101292

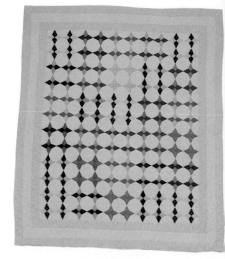

3101292

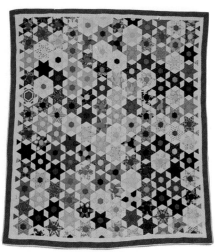

4101292

5101292

6101292

1101292 – LONE STAR; 45" x 45"; blues, pink with blue, pink & gold prints; all cotton; made in Minnesota in 1991; machine pieced, hand quilted; low loft batting, blue & pink star is on soft blue background which is channel quilted by hand; French fold bias binding has mitered corners. $172.00

2101292 – TRIP AROUND THE WORLD; 74" x 102"; red, white & blue, unbleached muslin back; all 100% cotton except the white on top, which is 50% cotton, 50% polyester; made in California in 1991; machine pieced, hand tied in every corner; extra loft batting, prewashed fabrics. $201.00

3101292 – PONTIAC STAR; 84" x 94"; variety of colors in the star design on white background with pink border; 100% cotton; made in Iowa in 1990; machine pieced, hand quilted; Mountain Mist Traditional batting. $316.00

4101292 – FRENCH BOUQUET; 87" x 98"; white with red border, multicolored fabrics; cotton & cotton/polyester blends; made in Arkansas in 1992; hand pieced & quilted; double bias binding, polyester batting. $259.00

5101292 – DELECTABLE MOUNTAIN; 19" x 19"; 14 traditional Amish colors, wine background; 100% cotton; made in Michigan in 1991; machine pieced, hand quilted with wine quilting thread; center quilted with folk art flower triangles with clam shells; back is Mule Shoe Sweet Feed sacking. $86.00

6101292 – DOUBLE WEDDING RING; 94" x 107"; dusty blue & dusty pink with off-white background; cotton/polyester blend fabrics; made in Missouri in 1992; machine pieced, hand quilted; Dacron™ batting, heart quilting design. $448.00

7101292 – DOUBLE IRISH CHAIN; 87" x 103"; yellow & light green, small yellow rosebuds print with orange flowers; 100% cotton; 100% perma-press bleached muslin; made in Hawaii in 1991; machine pieced & quilted; heart quilted in center of chain pattern, 9 patch corners, 4" borders, polyester batting, double fold binding borders. $259.00

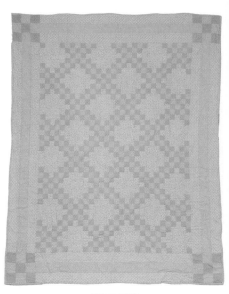

7101292

1111292

2111292

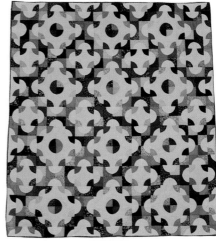

3111292

4111292

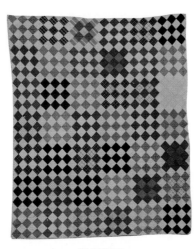

5111292

6111292

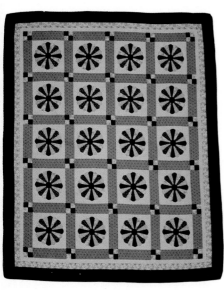

7111292

1111292 – ONTARIO LAKES; 90" x 105"; taupe, light green, mauve, cream; cottons (some batiks); made in California in 1991; machine pieced & quilted; cotton classic batting; done in soft pastel colors, featuring batik in block centers and on backing, machine quilted in a wave pattern. $431.00

2111292 – HEARTS – HEARTS – HEARTS!; 42" x 54"; red prints, background white with mini red print, bright blue accent & backing; 100% cottons; made in Virginia in 1992; machine pieced, hand quilted; red quilted hearts in the hearts; solid blue back shows quilting, double bias binding. $126.00

3111292 – AROUND THE WORLD WITH MY SCRAPBAG; 86" x 96"; off-white background with assorted scraps/colors; all cotton; made in Kansas in 1992; machine pieced, hand quilted; Mountain Mist batting w/polyester/cotton blend backing; double binding; flower quilted in off-white. $276.00

4111292 – DRESDEN PLATE; 88" x 104"; shades of brown & tan on cream background with a touch of peach, blue & pink; all cotton fabrics; made in Kansas in 1987; machine pieced, hand quilted; polyester batting, won a blue ribbon at county fair in 1987. $345.00

5111292 – CHECKERBOARD; 64" x 75"; turkey red, navy blues, chambray & black shirting fabrics; 100% cotton fabrics; maker unknown (early 1900's?); made in Atlanta, GA area; hand pieced & quilted; relatively good condition for age of quilt; turkey red squares in need of repair, original binding intact & in good shape, a few rust & water stains on back of quilt; owner purchased at an estate auction. $201.00

6111292 – ENCIRCLED TULIP; 88" x 103"; burgundy, pink & yellow w/white; all cotton top, poly-cotton backing; made in Kansas in 1991; machine pieced, hand quilted & appliqued; Mountain Mist batting; double binding with rounded corners. $448.00

7111292 – NOONDAY LILY; 80" x 92"; pink lilies w/green stems on off-white; cotton & cotton/polyester blends; made in California in 1992; hand appliqued & quilted; polyester batting. $391.00

1121292

2121292

3121292

4121292

5121292

6121292

1121292 – HOME IS MY HEART; 80" x 86"; on natural muslin with red print hearts & navy print houses; 100% cotton; made in Tennessee in 1992; hand appliqued and quilted with small quilting stitches; polyester batting. $460.00

2121292 – THE SWAN; 23" x 32"; multicolored satins (beige, light brown/gold, light blue & more), black border & trim; made in 1988 in South Carolina; hand pieced & quilted; made to look like a stained glass window with a swan on the lake in the center. $144.00

3121292 – TRIP AROUND THE WORLD; 86" x 92"; peach & blue; cotton; made in Alabama in 1992; machine pieced, hand quilted; polyfil batting; sheet lining, double quilted by hand. $299.00

4121292 – BROKEN STAR; 81" x 89"; green, red, off-white; prewashed cotton; made in Wisconsin in 1992; machine pieced & quilted using heirloom machine quilting techniques developed by Harriet Hargrave; hand-stitched binding, preshrunk cotton/polyester blend batting $460.00

5121292 – BABY GRANDMOTHER'S FAN; 36" x 50"; pink & blue with multicolored baby prints on white background; cotton with a little polyester; made in Kansas in 1992; machine pieced, hand quilted; crib quilt or wallhanging, polyester/cotton backing, polyester batting, pattern is a small Grandmother's Fan design with lace around each fan. $109.00

6121292 – LOG CABIN BARN RAISING; 81" x 102"; teal green & rose; cotton; made in Illinois in 1992; machine pieced & quilted; polyester batting. $288.00

7121292 – INDIAN ARROWHEAD; 94" x 106"; lavender floral with dark purple solid contrast; 100% cotton; made in Connecticut in 1992; machine pieced, hand quilted in purple thread; polyester batting, double bias binding, muslin backing. $345.00

7121292

1131292

2131292

3131292

4131292

5131292

6131292

7131292

1131292 – LOG CABIN; 86" x 112"; multicolored dark polyester/cotton fabrics; made in Missouri in 1991; machine pieced, hand quilted; polyester batting. $402.00

2131292 – AMISH TRIPLE IRISH CHAIN; 85" x 108"; red, maroon & black; 100% prewashed cotton; made in Illinois in 1992; machine pieced, hand quilted with traditional Amish feather wreath and feather border patterns; backing is black, small quilting stitches. $748.00

3131292 – PRAIRIE QUEEN; 87" x 105"; multicolored with peach, purple, yellow, blue & greens; cotton/polyester blend fabrics; made in Missouri in 1992; machine pieced & quilted; polyester batting. $230.00

4131292 – HAVEN'T WE ET BEFORE; 38" x 46"; black, white & red; prewashed cotton fabrics; made in California in 1991; machine pieced & quilted; polyester batting; after a Maryellen Hopkins design from the book *Baker's Dozen Doubled*; Kasuri Dye Works Japanese fabric, Japanese calligraphy & lobster prints, colorfast, hanging pocket. $299.00

5131292 – ARIZONA POPPY; 42" x 42"; yellows, oranges, reds against off-white background with black accents; all cotton; made in Arizona in 1992; machine pieced & quilted; polyester batting. $345.00

6131292 – BEST WISHES; 48" x 48"; shades of mauve, navy, green, white on matching printed ground, backing mauve to match; cotton; made in Michigan in 1990; Mountain Mist polyester batting, hanging sleeve, border quilted. $217.00

7131292 – NURSERY RHYMES; 82" x 88"; beige, chocolate brown, black; cotton & cotton/polyester blends; made in Illinois in 1988; machine appliqued, pieced & quilted; 14 nursery rhyme motifs, prairie point edging on three sides, won a 2nd place ribbon at Illinois State Fair in 1988. $98.00

1151292

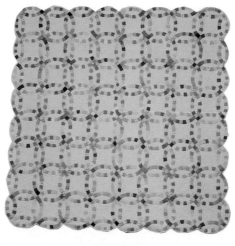

2151292

3151292

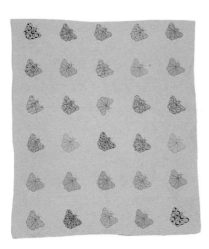

4151292

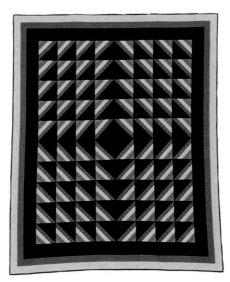

5151292

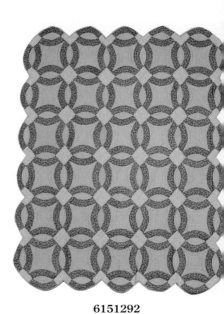

6151292

7151292

1151292 – EIGHT POINTED STAR; 41" x 41"; blue with cream background; cotton/polyester blends; made in Missouri in 1992; plain block has house quilted in it, polyester batting. $70.00

2151292 – DOUBLE WEDDING RING; 104" x 107"; light colors of pink, blue, green & peach with cream background; cotton/polyester blends; made in Missouri in 1992; machine pieced, hand quilted; polyester batting. $431.00

3151292 – LOVE RING; 84" x 100"; browns, off-white; 100% cotton; made in Nebraska in 1991; machine pieced, hand quilted; polyester batting, coordinating brown print backing. $518.00

4151292 – BUTTERFLY APPLIQUE; 69" x 78"; off-white background, faded pink sashing; cotton; history of quilt not known, possibly made 1920's or 1930's, bought at auction, in great condition except for one age spot; appliqued butterflies, hand quilted, thin batting. $230.00

5151292 – ROMAN STRIPE; 75" x 89"; black, purple, pink, blue & green; polyester/cotton blend fabrics; made in Indiana in 1986; machine pieced, hand quilted; black backing, never used. $230.00

6151292 – DOUBLE WEDDING RING; 97" x 118"; rose, wine, light corners, beige background; cotton/polyester blend fabrics; made in Illinois in 1992; machine pieced, hand quilted; polyester batting, a traditional pattern in the king size. $247.00

7151292 – WEDDING RING; 78" x 96"; light blue solid, yellow print, white broadcloth; broadcloth fabric; made in 1992 in Tennessee; hand pieced & quilted; polyester batting, bleached sheeting lining. $345.00

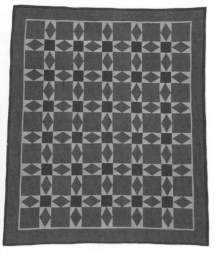

1161292

2161292

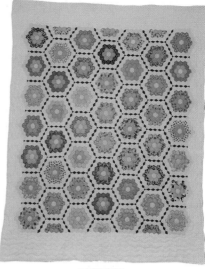

3161292

4161292

5161292

6161292

1161292 – UNKNOWN STAR; 75" x 86"; red, medium blue, light blue; 100% cotton solids; made in Washington in 1991; machine pieced, hand quilted; cotton batting. $345.00

2161292 – OCEAN WAVES; 85" x 105"; more than 25 traditional Amish colors used, black back; beautifully quilted; the border is a combination of feather and cable quilting patterns; machine pieced, hand quilted; prewashed fabrics used. $748.00

3161292 – MARTHA WASHINGTON FLOWER GARDEN; 80" x 102"; off-white background, multi-colored flowers with green diamonds; 100% cotton; made in Iowa in 1979; machine pieced, hand quilted; Mountain Mist batting, mulicolored flower pattern could fit any decor. $316.00

4161292 – SCRAP BASKET; 86" x 98"; beige background, floral & brown border with mulicolored baskets; 65% cotton/35% polyester fabric; made in Illinois in 1985-92; machine pieced, hand quilted; polyester batting, medium weight quilt, back of quilt is beige–same as front. $316.00

5161292 – OVERALL SAM; 34" x 45"; natural muslin with country-toned primary colors; cotton; made in Minnesota in 1991; machine pieced, hand appliqued, quilted and embroidered; polyester batting, all figures bottonhole-stitched in black for a 1930's look. $161.00

6161292 – SCRAP QUILT; 84" x 84"; predominately blue with multicolored alternating blocks; cottons; made in Maryland in 1991; machine pieced, hand quilted; original made with sections of early 1900's scrap quilt, Mountain Mist batting. $247.00

7161292 – DRESDEN PLATE; 78" x 95"; mauve backing, plates on solid mauve; cotton/polyester blends; made in Arkansas in 1990; machine pieced & appliqued, hand quilted; polyester batting; can use the reverse side for solid mauve look, double binding. $259.00

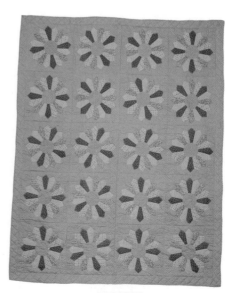

7161292

1171292

2171292

3171292

4171292

5171292

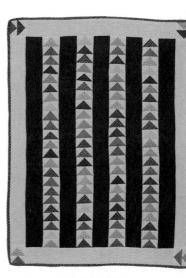

6171292

7171292

1171292 – UNKNOWN; 85" x 101"; pink & white with yellow, lavender and green solids & prints 100% cotton, muslin lining; top made c. 1940 in New York; hand pieced & bound, machine quilted in 1991; quilt was pieced from a kit and has not been used. $201.00

2171292 – LOG CABIN; 94" x 102"; blue on blue, navy, blue lining; cotton; made in Alabama in 1991 machine pieced, hand quilted on each side of seam; polyester batting, sheet lining, light-to-dark print $402.00

3171292 – MINIATURE GRANDMOTHER'S FLOWER GARDEN; 72" x 72"; pastel prints on whit background; 100% cotton; made in Alabama in 1991; hand pieced & quilted; polyester batting. $402.00

4171292 – STARSHINE AROUND THE WORLD; 46" x 46"; blues, aqua & green; cotton & cotton/polyester blends; made in North Dakota in 1992; machine pieced & quilted; made with quilt-as you-go method by Arlene Boyd from Summer 1989 *American Quilter* magazine, backgrounds stippl quilted by machine making a brocade effect, binding is rainbow-silver lamé. $115.00

5171292 – FRIETCHIE STAR; 79" x 87"; dark & light browns with brown/white floral print on dar brown background, floral print on the scallops; cotton/polyester blends; made in Missouri in 198(machine pieced & quilted; bias tape binding, large scallops are hand appliqued, polyfil polyester batting closely quilted, light brown lining. $201.00

6171292 – FLYING GEESE; 32" x 41"; blue & white; 100% cotton calico; made in California in 1992 machine pieced, hand quilted; lots of hand quilting; may be used as crib quilt or wallhanging. $167.00

7171292 – TRELLIS ROSE; 82" x 98"; mauve, rose & white; cotton; made in Kansas in 1991 machine pieced, hand quilted & appliqued; Mountain Mist batting, mitered corners, double binding $391.00

1181292

2181292

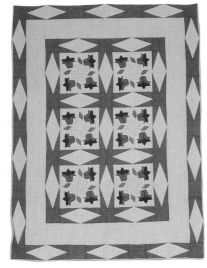

3181292

4181292

5181292

6181292

181292 – PINWHEEL; 57" x 58"; soft country & navy blues with splashes of red & gray; antique
cotton fabrics; unknown maker of top; hand pieced & quilted; Mountain Mist low-loft batting, top bought
nd quilted by owner in 1991. $230.00

181292 – SUNBONNET SUE & FARMER BILL; 41" x 50"; yellow checked border with multicol-
red fabrics on applique; cotton & polyester blends; made in Illinois in 1992; hand appliqued & quilted;
erfect size for crib quilt. $86.00

181292 – TULIP APPLIQUE; 81" x 104"; rose on off-white; cotton & cotton/polyester blend fab-
cs; made in Illinois in 1990; hand quilted, machine pieced & appliqued. $397.00

181292 – HOSPITALITY; 70" x 78"; off-white muslin background with yellow print & solid green;
0% cotton; made in Tennessee in 1992; hand appliqued & quilted, machine pieced; low-loft batting; the
neapple is a symbol of hospitality; edge of quilt is bound in the yellow pineapple print in a dainty scal-
p, this can be a bed or wall quilt. $345.00

181292 – MINIATURE LOG CABIN; 31" x 31"; blue & mauve; cotton; made in Illinois in 1992;
achine pieced, hand quilted; can be used as wallhanging or table centerpiece. $109.00

181292 – SUNSHINE & SHADOW; 85" x 84"; wide border of cobalt blue with purples, corals,
eens & blues; cotton; made in the early 1970's by Amish in Midwest; hand quilted with black thread;
ool batting; purchased from an Amish lady who said she was only selling it because it had some wool
it & would require dry cleaning. $695.00

181292 – SWEETHEART; 80" x 94"; mauve on off-white; cotton; made in Illinois in 1990; hand
ppliqued, machine pieced; lovely valentine look, off-white shadow print on front and off-white backing;
ver used. $690.00

7181292

1191292

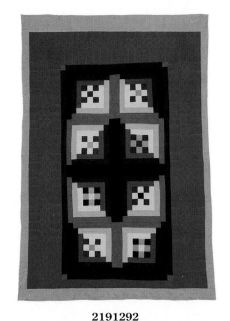

2191292

3191292

4191292

5191292

6191292

7191292

1191292 – QUILTED BLOCKS; 40" x 40"; tan, rust & brown; cotton/polyester blend fabrics; mad
in Arkansas in 1992; machine pieced & appliqued, hand quilted; polyester battting, has rod pocke
$86.00

2191292 – UNNAMED; 65" x 97"; tan backing, front colors are blue, brown, black, yellows & pink
100% cotton; made in Wales; machine pieced, hand quilted; polyester batting, design inspired by trad
tional Celtic knotwork, combines Celtic & Amish designs. $230.00

3191292 – BILLY BOY; 41" x 51"; blue pinchecked border, multicolored applique; cotton & co
ton/polyester blends; made in 1992 in Illinois; hand quilted & appliqued; crib quilt. $86.00

4191292 – LOG CABIN; 54" x 54"; shades of dusty blue; cotton/polyester blends; made in Illinois i
1992; machine pieced, hand quilted. $172.00

5191292 – HEN AND CHICKS; 42" x 42"; off-white background, many pastels – blue, pink & beig
cotton & cotton/polyester; made in Minnesota in 1992; polyester batting, many fabrics make up this pa
tel quilt, heavily quilted with swag border & other motifs in larger spaces of quilt, suitable as wall quil
table cover or for baby. $172.00

6191292 – STAR; 48" x 48"; antique reds & greens; cotton & cotton/polyester blends; made i
North Carolina in 1992; machine pieced, hand quilted; polyfil batting, may be used as wallhanging o
table cloth. $115.00

7191292 – TREES; 75" x 75"; blue & white; 100% cotton; unknown maker, the date "1913" embro
dered on quilt; origin Midwest; machine pieced, hand quilted; mint condition antique quilt densel
quilted; trees have sharp points and are made of a beautiful country blue print. $1,725.00

96

1010393

2010393

3010393

4010393

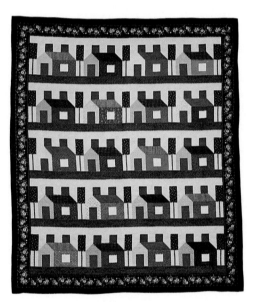

5010393

6010393

7010393

1010393 – LOG CABIN - BARN RAISING; 48" x 48"; browns, yellows, golds with bright salmon accents, coordinating brown/blue floral backing; cottons & cotton/polyester blends; made in Upstate New York in 1984; machine pieced, tied in gold-colored cotton twist, hand finished binding (straight grain, baby yellow checks); polyester batting. $70.00

2010393 – HEARTS & SHAMROCKS – SINGLE IRISH CHAIN; 42" x 48"; medium blue, peach, rust, background is a tiny flowered print, blue & peach on off-white; all prewashed cotton fabrics; made in North Carolina in 1989; machine pieced, hand quilted & appliqued; a traditional Irish Chain combined w/appliqued hearts in soft, soothing colors and lots of hand quilting in cable & shamrock motifs; originally used as teacher's sample, sleeve for hanging. $150.00

3010393 – HAWAIIAN SAMPLER; 88" x 88"; navy blue, off-white background; 100% cotton; made in Florida in 1984; hand appliqued & quilted; pattern was from a series featured in *Quilter's Newsletter* magazine; won a red ribbon in 1985 Florida State Fair; never used. $690.00

4010393 – HEXAGON STAR; 77" x 92"; stars of bright colors, each a different print, set with off-white broadcloth hexagons; cotton and cotton/polyester blends; made in 1982 in Illinois; all hand made; edge of border shaped. $575.00

5010393 – PEOPLE PLACES; 86" x 100"; rose, maroon, blue & indigo cottons with a light blue calico back; made in Pennsylvania in 1992; machine pieced, hand quilted; polyester batting. $448.00

6010393 – SAMPLER; 62" x 76"; multicolored cotton; maker unknown; made in Nebraska in 1930's; machine & hand pieced, hand appliqued & quilted; the top is from the 1930's, but newly quilted. $460.00

7010393 – TULIPS & STAR; 79" x 93"; blue; percale & broadcloth, muslin lining; made in Missouri in 1992; machine pieced, hand quilted & appliqued; polyester batting; original random quilting on the border. $334.00

97

1020393

2020393

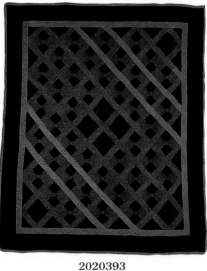

3020393

4020393

5020393

6020393

1020393 – GARDEN PATHS; 83" x 98"; green, burgundy & white; cotton & cotton/polyester; made in New Mexico in 1992; machine pieced & quilted; polyester batting. $276.00

2020393 – AMISH BOW TIES; 67" x 77"; black, blue, burgundy, blue bowties on black background w/burgundy lattice; cotton; maker not known (initials on quilt), made January 8, 1911 in Ohio; hand quilted; this is a quilt within a quilt…older Bowtie is inside this quilt, quilted by the piece, a few paint stains. $1840.00

3020393 – DRESDEN PLATE; 89" x 106"; old rose w/beige, one fan is light brown; all cotton; made in Kansas in 1987 (never used); hand quilted & appliqued; hearts are quilted in each corner of block and in sashing; mitered corners, double binding. $368.00

4020393 – FRAMED FLOWERS; 72" x 86"; bright jewel color frames for printed squares; cottons & blends; made in Illinois in 1991; hand and machine pieced, hand quilted; polyester batting; prairie point edge. $460.00

5020393 – TRIANGLE SQUARES; 81" x 92"; dark scraps w/burgundy borders; 100% cotton; made in Pennsylvania in 1990; hand quilted. $776.00

6020393 – SHOO-FLY; 76" x 88"; white background, dominate red pattern in shoo-fly with small white hearts; cotton; made in New York in 1992; machine pieced, hand quilted; polyester batting. $368.00

7020393 – CARPENTER'S WHEEL; 88" x 103"; blue, red w/off-white background; 100% cotton; made in Tennessee in 1990; hand pieced & quilted w/feather design; Mountain Mist batting. $899.00

7020393

98

1030393

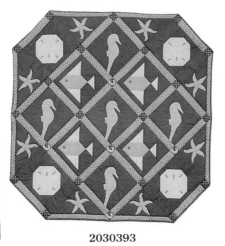

2030393

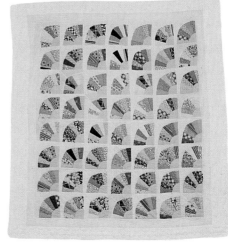

3030393

4030393

5030393

6030393

7030393

1030393 – DRESDEN PLATE; 94" x 94"; off-white print background, peach & brown plate spokes, brown border, plate & off-white print backing, accent brown sateen; perma press cottons; recently made in California; machine pieced, plates hand appliqued; honorable mention San Diego Quilt Show. $460.00

2030393 – WINDOWS OF THE SEA; 52" x 52"; Williamsburg blue background w/peach, tan, & natural dots, stripes & calico; all cotton; made in Pennsylvania in 1991; machine pieced, hand quilted & appliqued; original design w/detailed sand dollars, starfish, seahorses & fish all outline quilt. Seahorse tails wrap around sashing squares. $230.00

3030393 – FAN QUILT; 85" x 90"; print fan blades on cream background w/white border; cotton; made in Iowa in 1989; machine pieced, hand quilted; top is early 1930's prints; quilt never used. $242.00

4030393 – TREE OF LIFE; 86" x 96"; country blue, white, yellows, green, brown, reds, orange; cotton/polyester blends; made in Indiana in 1989; all handmade; polyester batting; prize winner in county fair. $1035.00

5030393 – TRIP AROUND THE WORLD; 85" x 107"; light, medium & dark greens & off-white; cotton and some cotton/polyester blends; made in Indiana in 1992; machine pieced by quilt owner, hand quilted by Amish in the popular diamond shape; polyester batting. $288.00

6030393 – DOUBLE IRISH CHAIN; 80" x 96"; peach & medium brown prints, peach background, plain peach lining; 100% cotton; made in Hawaii in 1992; machine pieced & quilted (quilted around chain and quilted design in center of chain); 9 patch corners; polyester batting, double fold binding; 4" borders. $259.00

7030393 – TRIP AROUND THE WORLD; 92" x 108"; multicolored w/blue border; cotton; made in South Carolina in 1989; machine pieced, hand quilted; polyester batting. $575.00

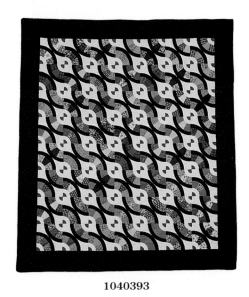

1040393

2040393

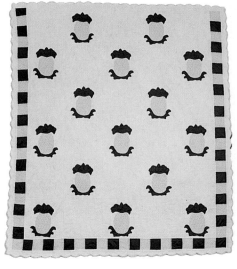

3040393

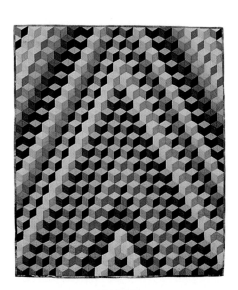

4040393

5040393

6040393

1040393 – GYPSY TRAIL; 84" x 95"; red centers on white, multicolored blocks; cotton and cotton/polyester blends; made in Illinois in 1979; the pattern is a double fan; hand & machine pieced, hand quilted. $402.00

2040393 – TREE OF LIFE; 76" x 88"; blue, green, gold & red on white; cotton; made in Illinois in 1975; hand appliqued & quilted; polyester batting; the applique is done in brown, red, blues, green & golds; the quilting has a feather and clam shell border around the center; bound in green. $1035.00

3040393 – PONTIAC STAR; 90" x 108"; off-white backing, assorted colors, predominate color blue; cotton and cotton/polyester blends; made in Arkansas in 1992; hand pieced & quilted; double bias binding; polyester batting. $288.00

4040393 – TOWER OF BABEL/TUMBLING BLOCKS; 51" x 59"; a spectrum of solid Amish colors; 100% cotton; made in Pennsylvania in 1991; machine pieced & quilted; this design is a copy of an 1860 Ohio Amish Tumbling Blocks; exhibited in juried quilt show in 1991 in Pennsylvania. $345.00

5040393 – BEARS PAW OR KANSAS TROUBLE; 88" x 89"; orchid & off-white; cotton fabrics; made in Oklahoma in 1988-89; lap hand quilted, machine pieced; Fairfield poly-fil low-loft batting; quilt never used. $632.00

6040393 – PEACH FANTASY; 84" x 104"; peach, green, off-white; cotton and cotton/polyester blends; made in Pennsylvania in 1991; machine pieced, hand quilted; peach backing, double edge binding. $402.00

7040393 – HOSPITALITY; 70" x 78"; off-white, yellow print, solid green; 100% cotton; hand appliqued & quilted, machine pieced; low-loft batting; the pineapple is a symbol of hospitality & friendship; this can be a bed or wall quilt; edge of quilt is bound in the yellow pineapple print in a dainty scallop. $288.00

7040393

1050393

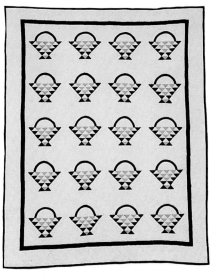

2050393

3050393

4050393

5050393

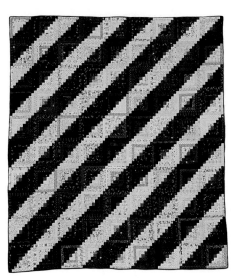

6050393

7050393

1050393 – BLOCKS IN BLOCKS; 80" x 90"; multicolored blocks on a print blue & white small flower background; cotton; made in Iowa in 1989; machine pieced top, hand quilted; Mountain Mist batting; old top recently hand quilted by one person. $264.00

2050393 – CHERRY BASKET; 84" x 103"; small print navy and medium blue, white background; cottons; made in Ohio in 1992; machine pieced, hand quilted & appliqued; quilting pattern of feather circles, flowers, hearts & shells; harmonizing blue prints contrast with the white background, bound with the navy small print. $385.00

3050393 – STAR GLOW; 88" x 102"; brown & tan w/brown chintz accent, backing in tiny brown print; 100% cotton; made in Alabama in 1992; machine pieced & quilted; based on Star Glow pattern featured in *Quilter's Newsletter* magazine in 1992; Hobbs poly down batting. $402.00

4050393 – LILY OF THE VALLEY; 90" x 91"; white broadcloth, green & rose cotton/polyester blends; made in Arkansas in 1989; hand pieced & quilted; either side can be used, since the backing and binding are both white. $259.00

5050393 – TUMBLIN' STAR; 80" x 94"; beige & brown; cotton; made in Alabama in 1991; machine pieced, hand quilted on each side of seam; polyester batting, beige lining; never used. $288.00

6050393 – LOG CABIN - STRAIGHT FURROW; 82" x 93"; mixed lights and darks; mostly cotton fabrics; recently made in Illinois; hand & machine pieced, hand quilted; polyester batting; extra long for a generous pillow tuck. $460.00

7050393 – PYRAMID; 82" x 96"; dark blue & red print calico, white in star; calico prints; made in Tennessee in 1992; hand pieced & quilted; polyester batting, bleached sheeting lining. $345.00

1060393

2060393

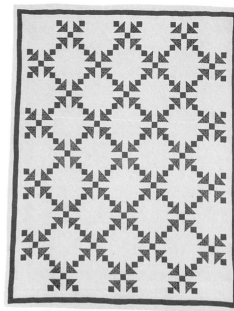

3060393 ↗

4060393

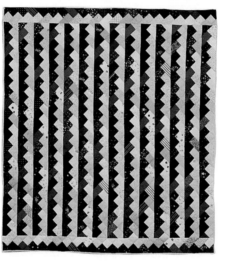

5060393

6060393

1060393 – SAMPLER; 87" x 93"; browns and off-white; 100% cotton; made in Wisconsin in 1992; machine pieced and quilted; cotton batting. $374.00

2060393 – CRAZY QUILT; 46 " x 66"; multicolored solid & print silks; maker unknown, probably made between 1880-1900, area of origin unknown; hand appliqued & embroidered; very little wear on this silk crazy quilt. $230.00

3060393 – GRANDMOTHER'S PRIDE; 90" x 110"; light beige, dark violet solid & print; muslin, cotton/polyester; made in Illinois in 1989; machine pieced, hand quilted; beige background; polyester batting. $316.00

4060393 – "IT WAS IN THE STARS"; 47" x 54"; several shades of blue w/cranberry border; cottons; made in Pennsylvania in 1991; hand pieced, quilted & appliqued; this quilt–a pictorial of Columbus and his ships–was made for *Quilter's Newsletter* "Discover America" contest and has been featured in shows; polyester batting. $1150.00

5060393 – FRIENDSHIP BRAID; 62" x 70"; multicolored: red, white, yellow, pink, blue, green, brown, black, prints & solids; all cotton top & backing; made in California in 1990; machine pieced, hand quilted; traditional batting, pastel pink cotton backing & binding. $374.00

6060393 – SOMEWHERE IN THE GARDEN; 40" x 40"; country blues, roses & cream florals, backing solid cream; 100% cottons; made in Virginia in 1992; machine pieced, hand quilted; polyester batting; one-of-a-kind quilting stitches; double bias bound w/mitered corners. $98.00

7060393 – NAVAJO; 90" x 100"; 8 different greens from very light to dark, blue-green overtones; 100% cotton fabrics; made in Northwest Territories in 1990; machine pieced; tied w/embroidery floss; polyfil low-loft batting. $402.00

7060393

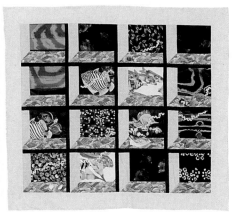

1070393

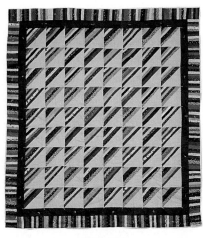

2070393

3070393

4070393

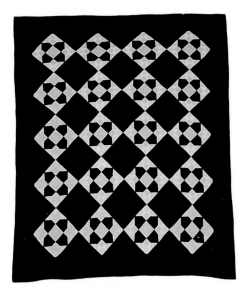

5070393

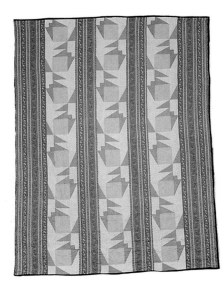

6070393

7070393

1070393 – WATER WINDOWS/ATTIC WINDOWS; 40" x 35"; beige, blue & yellow; fabric is 100% cotton; made in Indiana in 1991; machine pieced, tacked; embellishments include rocks, fish bone, shells & sequins; treasures gleaned from a Cape Cod vacation are glued on "window sills"; backing material is brightly colored beach umbrellas; polyester batting. $147.00

2070393 – (AMISH) SUNSHINE & SHADOWS; 92" x 101"; yellow, gold, brown, rust, touches of dark green, teal; cottons & polyester blends; made in Minnesota in 1992; machine pieced, tied w/natural color string (not yarn); polyester batting, cotton muslin natural color backing. $144.00

3070393 – SAMPLER; 40" x 40"; light & dark blue, light & dark rose; 100% cotton; made in New Jersey in 1991; machine pieced, hand quilted & appliqued; low-loft batting; lots of quilting. $161.00

4070393 – ATTIC WINDOWS - EAGLE; 36" x 36"; navy, red & off-white; all cotton; made in South Carolina in 1992-93; machine pieced, hand quilted; polyester low-loft batting; hanging sleeve on back; plenty of quilting in the ditch plus star designs in the border. $86.00

5070393 – WEATHERVANE; 80" x 100"; black w/light blue & violet, black backing, black thread; cotton; made in Iowa by Amish in 1952; top is hand & machine pieced, hand quilted; small quilting stitches, thin polyester batting, spiderweb quilting, black binding. $402.00

6070393 – TULIP GARDEN; 78" x 92"; peach, green & muslin; cotton & cotton/polyester blends; made in Arkansas in 1988; machine pieced & quilted in vertical ivy pattern running with the vertical tulip & border print rows; handmade binding in dark green. $100.00

7070393 – LOVE KNOT MEDALLIONS; 95" x 105"; unbleached muslin & multicolored calicoes; all cotton; made in Illinios in 1992; hand & machine pieced, hand quilted; this is a blend of large & small medallions pieced in muslin & dozens of softly bright calico prints; Mountain Mist traditional weight poly-fil batting, muslin back, pieced border of triangular points. $897.00

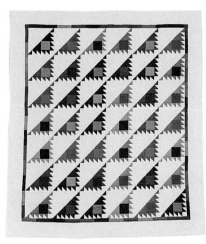

1080393

2080393

3080393

4080393

5080393

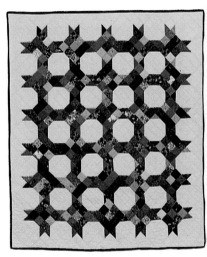

6080393

1080393 – SAWTOOTH; 75" x 84"; assorted prints, white background; cotton; made in Virginia in 1992; machine pieced, hand quilted w/rose design on each block; county fair blue ribbon winner. $345.00

2080393 – ART STAR/SAWTOOTH STAR; blues, purples & mauves; 100% cotton, some batik, hand dyed & hand painted; made in Texas in 1990; machine pieced, hand quilted; this quilt was in the *1991 American Quilts Calendar* by Lang Graphics and has been in *Quilting Today* magazine–it was also in the 1990 Quilt Festival Exhibit. $2875.00

3080393 – DOUBLE WEDDING RING; 88" x 102"; off-white background, the rings are a mixture of prints, blue squares; Dacron™ & cotton; made in Delaware in 1992; machine pieced, hand quilted & bound; polyester batting. $516.00

4080393 – DESERT SUNSET; 66" x 66"; black w/purples, turquoise & rosy tan; cotton & cotton blends; made in California in 1992; machine pieced, hand quilted; designed by maker; polyester batting, purple backing, heavily quilted. $345.00

5080393 – APPLIQUE WREATH; 90" x 98"; white, and red, blue, gold, green floral; cotton & cotton/polyester blends; made in Kansas in 1990; hand appliqued, bound & quilted. $460.00

6080393 – SNOWBALL; 51" x 58"; bright scraps on antique tan background; coordinated print backing; 100% cotton, prewashed; made in Louisiana in 1992; machine pieced & quilted tan cotton thread; batting is needlepunched cotton; quilt washed once to shrink batting; double thickness hand sewn binding. $230.00

7080393 – MELON MAGIC FROM QUILTMAKER #28; 54" x 66"; fruit print on black, red, green, tone-on-tone white; all cotton fabrics; made in Illinois in 1992; machine pieced, hand quilted w/red thread; Mountain Mist Quilt Lite batting; mitered corners; pieced back is large print watermelon plaid, complete w/ants; permanent matching red pocket attached, ready to hang. $426.00

7080393

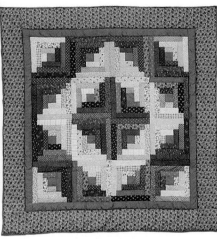

1090393

2090393

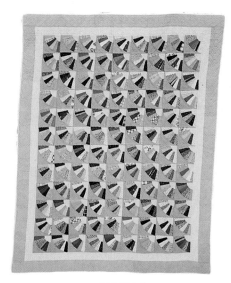

3090393

4090393

5090393

6090393

7090393

1090393 – LOG CABIN; 41" x 41"; this price includes a smaller 20" x 20" matching piece; the larger piece can be used as a bed topper, the smaller piece as a wall hanging; grayish blues; cotton & cotton/polyester blends; made in New York in 1992; machine pieced & quilted; both pieces have hanging sleeve. $155.00

2090393 – SUNSHINE & SHADOW; 38" x 38"; jewel tones of purple, blue & green w/black; made in Lancaster County, Pennsylvania c.1987; machine pieced, hand quilted; purchased by owner in the heart of Amish country at a farmhouse; quilt never used or hung. $115.00

3090393 – GRANDMOTHER'S FAN; 87" x 108"; assorted prints w/lavender & yellow background; cotton & cotton blends; made in Arkansas in 1989; hand pieced & quilted; white backing, double bias binding, good quilting. $288.00

4090393 – PINE TREE; 38" x 38"; dark green & beige; cotton; made in Minnesota in 1992; machine pieced, hand quilted; polyester batting; lots of quilting in pine trees; sleeve on the back for hanging; signed & dated. $172.00

5090393 – PASTEL FOUR PATCH; 34" x 41"; blue, pink, yellow & white; cotton/polyester blends; made in North Carolina in 1990; machine pieced & quilted; yellow & pink four patches alternated with blue patches; diagonal quilting, polyester batting; muslin backing; can be used as baby quilt or wallhanging. $92.00

6090393 – RYAN STAR; 85" x 100"; multicolored, purple, green, mauve; cotton/polyester blends; made in Missouri in 1992; machine pieced & quilted; polyester batting. $230.00

7090393 – 4 PATCH CORNER OHIO STAR; 90" x 114"; blue & white; 100% top quality cottons; made in Colorado in 1992; machine pieced, hand quilted; Cotton Classic batting (80% cotton, 20% polyester); heavily quilted w/lots of hearts, new double bias binding. $575.00

105

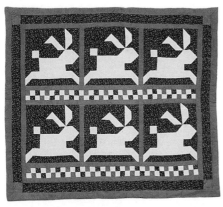

1100393

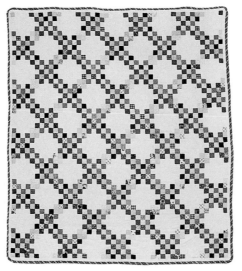

2100393

3100393

4100393

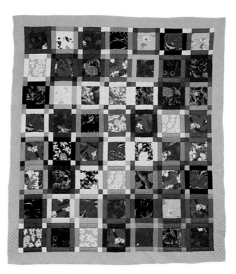

5100393

6100393

1100393 – BUNCH OF BUNNIES; 40" x 46"; salmon, purple & white flannel; all cotton; made in Maine in 1989; machine pieced, hand quilted; polyester batting; crib size made for first child after her birth but never used. $201.00

2100393 – DOUBLE IRISH CHAIN; 88" x 100"; cream background, red, blue; cotton & cotton/polyester; made in California in 1989; machine pieced, hand quilted; polyester batting. $345.00

3100393 – FANS FANS FANS; 38" x 39"; gray & navy; cotton & cotton/polyester blends; made in Florida in 1990; hand pieced & quilted; this fan quilt was the result of having a lot of fabric left over from other projects! $104.00

4100393 – 8 POINT STAR PATTERN; 80" x 94"; yellow background, pale green strip, blue print border, multicolors; cotton; made in Missouri in 1990 (top is from the 1950's); machine pieced, hand quilted. $282.00

5100393 – HAWAII SQUARES; 86" x 97"; orange border w/multicolored bright squares; cotton and cotton/poly blends; made in Ohio in 1992; machine pieced, hand quilted; polyester batting; all print squares except for two from Hawaii; the quilting is in a variety of geometric patterns and gridwork that makes this quilt look attractive on the back as well. $345.00

6100393 – MONKEY WRENCH; 73" x 97"; multicolored scrap quilt, dark blue sashing & backing; cotton; unknown maker, unknown date, probably made in Montana; machine pieced, hand quilted; poly-fil batting. $374.00

7100393 – DOUBLE WEDDING RING; 80" x 90"; yellow background & backing w/multicolored rings; cotton w/some cotton/polyester blends; made in Nebraska in 1989; hand pieced & quilted using an assymetrical bellflower motif; polyester batting; sleeve for hanging; this quilt took fourth in quilting category at 1989 Nebraska State Fair. $460.00

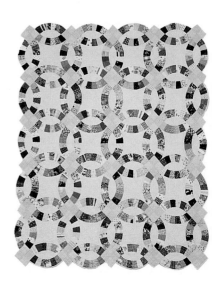

7100393

106

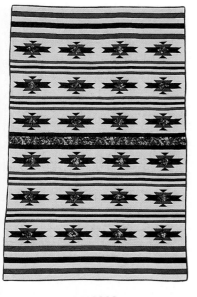

1110393

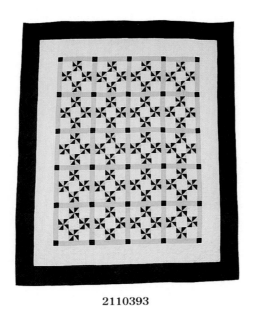

2110393

3110393

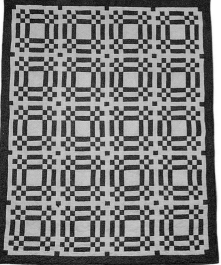

4110393

5110393

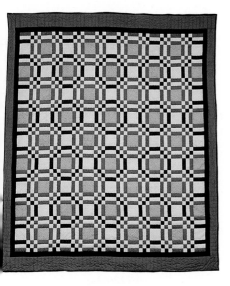

6110393

7110393

1110393 – INDIAN RUG; 65" x 96"; golden brown, dark blue, off-white, woods floral; made in Connecticut in 1992; cotton and cotton/polyester blends; machine pieced, hand quilted in seam to enhance design; all fabrics prewashed. $316.00

2110393 – FOUR-LEAF CLOVER; 90" x 104"; green/gold on off-white; cotton/polyester; made in Indiana in 1990; machine pieced, hand quilted; polyester batting, muslin backing. $397.00

3110393 – TEXAS STAR; 40" x 40"; red. blue, green & yellow on white background; 100% cotton; made in Texas in 1991; machine pieced, hand quilted; the print fabrics are old flour sacks purchased at a garage sale; low-loft batting; piecing was done by strip method. $109.00

4110393 – CORNER NINE PATCH; 87" x 103"; white & blue; cotton/polyester blend fabrics; made in Missouri in 1992; machine pieced & quilted; polyester batting. $230.00

5110393 – BEAR PAW; 51" x 42"; maroon, dusty pink, beige; 100% cotton; made in California in 1988; machine pieced & quilted; low-loft batting; hanging sleeve. $115.00

6110393 – MARINER'S COMPASS; 92" x 107"; blue, rust, chocolate, black on ecru background; cotton; made in Michigan in 1992; polyester batting; lots of feather quilting; echo quilting around compasses; double binding. $345.00

7110393 – IRIS JIG; 93" x 96"; blue; cotton/polyester blends; made in Missouri in 1992; machine pieced, hand quilted; polyester batting. $345.00

1120393

2120393

3120393

4120393

5120393

6120393

1120393 & 2120393 – DIAMOND IN A SQUARE - AMISH STAR; 24" x 24"; black, gray, purple, rose, blue, green, red; prewashed cotton; made in New York in 1990-91; machine pieced, lots of hand quilting; these two wallhangings are sold as a unit; the smaller Amish Star is 20" x 20"; both are hand quilted w/black thread and have low-loft polyester batting. $115.00

3120393 – SQUARE DREAMS; 92" x 98"; all cotton; made in Oregon in 1991; machine pieced & quilted; polyester batting. $345.00

4120393 – DOUBLE WEDDING RING; 77" x 101"; peach print & peach solid w/cream background; cotton/polyester batting; made in Missouri in 1991; machine pieced, hand quilted; polyester batting. $230.00

5120393 – SNOWBALL; 75" x 95"; red & yellow; cotton/polyester blends; made in Kentucky in 1992; hand pieced & quilted; Mountain Mist batting; outline quilting. $196.00

6120393 – PEACE IN OMAN; 51" x 51"; teals & peaches on black background; cotton; made in 1990-1991 in Virginia; hand & machine pieced, hand quilted; tumbling blocks pattern arranged in 6-point star formation; quilt was made during Persian Gulf conflict and is an attempt to bring together the symbols of warring cultures: the Arabic mosaic & the Jewish Star of David; hexagon 25½" per side (51" in diameter). $345.00

7120393 – DAHLIA; 96" x 110"; forest green w/peach print, off-white background; cotton/polyester blends; made in Missouri by Mennonites in 1992; machine pieced, hand quilted; Dacron™ batting; signed & dated. $437.00

7120393

1130393

2130393

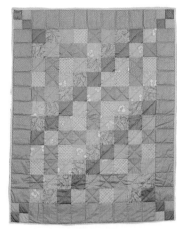

3130393

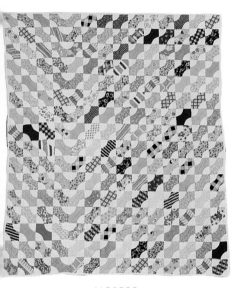

4130393

5130393

6130393

7130393

1130393 – POINSETTIA; 34" x 34"; predominate colors red, green & beige, back of quilt green floral; 100% cotton; made in New York in 1992; hand pieced & quilted; made from a pattern in *Quiltmaker* magazine; all new material has been washed; Hobbs batting. $288.00

2130393 – STREET LIGHTS; 86" x 102"; white, yellow, black & white check; cotton and cotton/polyester blends; made in Illinois in 1990; machine pieced, hand quilted; white background w/yellow corner lights w/black & white checked sidewalks; non-allergenic polyester batting. $316.00

3130393 – NINE PATCH; 33" x 41"; pastel pink, blue & mint; 100% cotton & cotton chintz; made in Georgia in 1992; machine pieced, hand quilted; solid mint border, pink binding, polyester batting, solid mint cotton backing. $172.00

4130393 – BOW TIE; 72" x 84"; white background w/scraps of many colors, including prints & some feed sacks; cotton; unknown maker c.1930, area of origin North Carolina; machine pieced, hand quilted; cotton batting; this quilt is a good representation of the prints & feed sacks used in the 1930's; good condition. $489.00

5130393 – GRAPE BASKET; 80" x 92"; blue & white; prewashed cotton; made in Texas in 1992; machine pieced & quilted; feather wreath quilting; Mountain Mist polyester batting. $345.00

6130393 – RENAISSANCE STAR; 36" x 36"; green, coral, off-white, multicolored; cottons; made in North Dakota in 1991; hand pieced & quilted; low-loft polyester batting; a red ribbon winner at ND State Fair in wallhanging category. $230.00

7130393 – EIGHT POINTED STAR; 77" x 94"; blue sashing, borders & backing–muslin background; cotton; made in Nebraska in 1930's or early 1940's, maker unknown; hand & machine pieced, hand quilted; cotton batting, never used. $345.00

1140393

2140393

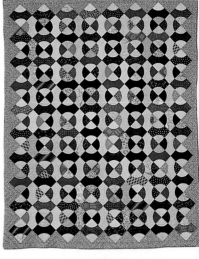

3140393

4140393

5140393

6140393

1140393 – CROSS STITCH PANSIES; 79" x 94"; white pansy cross stitch blocks alternated w/pink, pink back; all cotton; made by quilt owner's mother in 1961 in Minnesota; machine pieced, hand quilted & embroidered; this quilt has never been used. $345.00

2140393 – TWISTED STAR; 105" x 114"; black w/plain Amish colors: blues, aquas, greens & purples–light & dark; broadcloth poly/cotton (won't fade, shrink or wrinkle); made in 1992 by Amish in Pennsylvania; machine pieced, hand quilted w/fine stitches; new pattern w/feather quilting designs. $575.00

3140393 – MARBLE; 72" x 86"; dark & light fabrics, dark rose print border; cottons; made in Illinois in 1989; hand pieced & quilted; polyester batting. $345.00

4140393 – CHURN DASH; 72" x 86"; prints w/unbleached, set alternately w/gray print, pieced borders and print border; made in 1975 in Illinois; hand & machine pieced, hand quilted; polyester batting. $288.00

5140393 – FLYING GEESE; 66" x 76"; mustard gold & beige, bubblegum print backing; cotton; maker unknown; probably made in very early 1900's in North Carolina area; hand & machine pieced; hand quilted & embroidered (initials in some blocks); cotton batting; worn edges with some spots, but nicely quilted. $132.00

6140393 – IRIS FABRIC SAMPLER; 30" x 30"; purple, blue, yellow, green; 100% cottons; made in Virginia in 1992; machine pieced, hand quilted; the fabrics were chosen to complement the Iris print, corded binding, cable & lotus quilting designs in sashing & border, polyester batting, unbleached muslin backing. $115.00

7140393 – BLOSSOM OF SPRING; 49" x 55"; gray-greens & peaches; cottons; made in Pennsylvania in 1991; machine pieced, hand quilted; polyfil batting. $374.00

7140393

110

1150393

2150393

3150393

4150393

5150393

6150393

7150393

1150393 – BASKET & BOWS; 70" x 88"; light blues & mauve on white background; cotton; made in California in 1990; machine pieced, hand quilted & appliqued; soft pastel prints on white background; polyester batting; sleeve for hanging on back; bows are hand appliqued w/embroidery details. $600.00

2150393 – CRAZY QUILT; 57" x 79"; black w/mostly dark scraps; all velvet scrap quilt; made c.1890 probably in New York area; handmade; featherstitched and lazy-daisy embroidery, rich red backing fabric; good condition except for two or three patches which show the cracking of velvet; history unknown. $345.00

3150393 – SISTER'S STAR; 83" x 102"; peach, green, off-white; 100% cotton; made in New York state in 1991; machine pieced, free-motion machine quilted; polyester batting. $402.00

4150393 – ROMAN SQUARES; 62" x 81"; predominately navy & red w/yellow highlights; all pre-washed cotton; made in South Carolina in 1990; machine pieced, hand quilted; extensive quilting in ditch and through block squares. $345.00

5150393 – LOG CABIN VARIATION; 40" x 40"; pinks & blues; hand dyed cotton fabrics; made in South Carolina in 1989; machine pieced & quilted; original variation of Log Cabin block pattern; Mountain Mist batting. $172.00

6150393 – LONE STAR; 96" x 96"; different shades of blue with off-white, very tiny dot of mauve; cotton/polyester fabric; made in Kentucky in 1990; hand pieced & quilted; polyester batting; done in small design. $374.00

7150393 – SEMINISH QUILT #2; 46" x 62"; blue, purple, black, tan & scarlet; 100% cotton; made in Oregon in 1989; machine pieced, hand quilted (solid areas), hand tacked (patchwork areas); this quilt uses Seminole Indian patchwork in a modified Amish bars format, hence the hybrid name "Seminish"; has been featured in several shows (including AQS 1992) and pictured in Summer 1991 issue of *Quilt* magazine. $1035.00

111

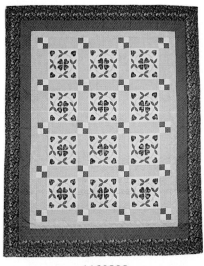

1160393

2160393

3160393

4160393

5160393

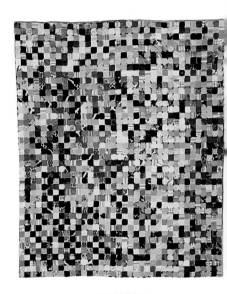

6160393

1160393 – BRIDAL WREATH; 104" x 88"; off-white background w/earth tone colors green, brown & rust; all cotton top, cotton/poly backing; made in Kansas in 1991; hand quilted & appliqued; Hobbs polyester batting. $391.00

2160393 – BEAR PAW; 92" x 109"; blue & white; broadcloth; made in Arkansas in 1991; machine pieced, hand quilted; polyester batting, white broadcloth backing; the paw is in royal blue; quilted around the seams, in the border and in the stripes. $259.00

3160393 – PINWHEEL CROSSES; 68" x 89"; variety of prints & solids against off-white background, pink edge, muslin backing; mostly 100% cotton fabrics, some from the 1930's, a few cotton/polyester blends (all prewashed); made in Illinois in 1992; machine pieced & quilted; low-loft poly batt; each cross made from 5 pinwheels; quilting on border is ribbon w/sprinkles of small pinwheels. $288.00

4160393 – LONE STAR; 94" x 108"; shades of burgundy on off-white; the prints are 100% cotton, the off-white is polyester & Dacron™; made in Missouri in 1992; machine pieced, hand quilted; polyester batting; this is a pattern handed down to the quiltmaker from her mother 40 years ago. $402.00

5160393 – KISSING DUCKS; 38" x 47"; blue, pink & yellow; cotton and cotton/polyester blends; made in Wisconsin in 1992; hand & machine quilted & appliqued, hand embroidered; polyester batting; excellent for boy or girl, crib or wallhanging. $70.00

6160393 – ENCIRCLED TULIP; 88" x 102"; shades of blue, rose, cream w/white background; all cotton; made in Kansas in 1991; machine pieced, hand quilted, tulips are hand appliqued; backing is cotton/polyester blend, batting polyester, mitered corners & double binding. $368.00

7160393 – SCRAP BAG SQUARES; 89" x 106"; multicolored 2½" squares; heavy cotton (denim, corduroy, etc.); made in Arizona in 1990; machine pieced, hand tied w/multicolored yarn; Mountain Mist polyester batting; reversible; hand sewn multicolored binding. $575.00

7160393

1170393

2170393

3170393

4170393

5170393

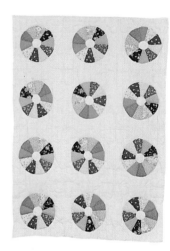

6170393

7170393

1170393 – BABY RAIL FENCE; 36" x 52"; pink & white; cotton fabric; made in Oregon in 1992; hand tied; polyester batting; rail fence of pink rosebuds on white background, medium pink feather and pink floral on mauve background; matching pink back. $40.00

2170393 – LOG CABIN; 96" x 123"; blue & white; cotton/polyester blends; made in Missouri in 1992; machine pieced & quilted; polyester batting. $230.00

3170393 – DINOSAUR; 45" x 62"; maroon background, dark blue print dinosaur (57" tall) with blue-gray lining and border to frame the picture; cotton & cotton/polyester blends; made in Texas in 1992; hand quilted, hand appliqued dinosaur. $75.00

4170393 – TIC-TAC-TOE; 43" x 43"; black & blue; cotton/polyester blend fabrics, corduroy & felt; made in Pennsylvania in 1992; machine pieced & quilted; polyfil batting; printed "x's" & "o's" are on the blue corduroy material w/black felt lines separating the "x's" & "o's" making a tic-tac-toe design. $55.00

5170393 – GARDEN MAZE/ SUNBURST WITH CHICKEN WIRE; 80" x 94"; pink w/white background; cotton; made in Missouri in 1985; hand pieced, quilted & appliqued; polyester batting; excellent hand work. $575.00

6170393 – NO NAME; 36" x 48"; multicolored prints on off-white background, lavender back; cotton fabrics with cotton/polyester backing; made in Pennsylvania in 1991; machine pieced, hand quilted & appliqued; Dacron™/polyester batting. $75.00

7170393 – ALBUM; 72" x 86"; backing & sashing are dark green, patches are multicolored scrap from the 1920's & 1930's. Solid red shows some fading; all cotton; made in 1920's in Oregon area, maker unknown; hand pieced and tied; batting is cotton; this quilt was found stored in a garage along with several others. $259.00

1180393

2180393

3180393

4180393

5180393

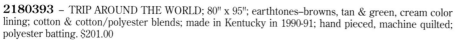

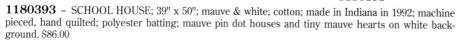

6180393

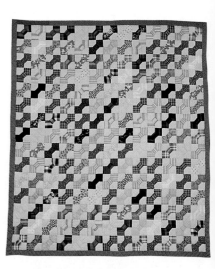

7180393

1180393 – SCHOOL HOUSE; 39" x 50"; mauve & white; cotton; made in Indiana in 1992; machine pieced, hand quilted; polyester batting; mauve pin dot houses and tiny mauve hearts on white background. $86.00

2180393 – TRIP AROUND THE WORLD; 80" x 95"; earthtones–browns, tan & green, cream color lining; cotton & cotton/polyester blends; made in Kentucky in 1990-91; hand pieced, machine quilted; polyester batting. $201.00

3180393 – STARS FROM STRIPES; 34" x 45"; green, raspberry & pink; cotton and cotton blends; made in Florida in 1989; hand pieced & quilted; polyester batting, hanging sleeve. $92.00

4180393 – BABY LAMB; 36" x 50"; pink w/white background, lambs are white w/colored embroidery; cotton/polyester blends; made in Kansas in 1992; machine pieced, hand quilted & embroidered; lambs are made of a soft cotton suede-like material which makes them stand out. $115.00

5180393 – DOGWOOD; 84" x 108"; pink w/jade green & white, yellow centers; all cotton w/polyester backing; made in Kansas in 1991; machine pieced, hand quilted & appliqued; quilted to look like a spider web; mitered corners & double binding. $380.00

6180393 – RUSSIAN GALLERY; 59" x 90"; dark, medium & bright brown, green & ochre; cotton; made in Hungary in 1988; machine pieced (patchwork) not quilted, silk-screen printed portraits assembled like icons then appliqued on dark background; shown on the Textile-Biennale of Hungary, 1992. $1150.00

7180393 – BOW TIE; 86" x 100"; various prints w/light blue background, white backing; cotton & cotton/polyester blends; made in Arkansas in 1992; hand pieced & quilted; polyester batting, double bias binding. $259.00

1190393

2190393

3190393

4190393

5190393

6190393

7190393

1190393 – AMISH; 34" x 34"; turkey red, gray-purple, purple, blue-green; cotton; made in Nebraska in 1992; machine pieced, hand quilted; polyfil poly batt; new quilt w/sleeve on back for hanging. $115.00

2190393 – GRANDMOTHER'S FLOWER GARDEN; 101" x 108"; light yellow background w/multi-colored flowers, backing is unbleached muslin; cotton & cotton blends; hand pieced in 1988 & hand quilted in 1992 in Colorado; perfect fit for king size bed. $460.00

3190393 – PIECED BASKET; 64" x 82"; pink, pink print, mauve & cream, coral lining; made in Kentucky in 1991; machine pieced & quilted (in ivy vine pattern); polyester batting; colors perfect for girl's room. $172.00

4190393 – FLOWER GARDEN; 65" x 82"; green/white with 12 blocks of various colored flowers; all cotton; made by owner's grandmother in 1932 (date embroidered into quilt) in Kansas; all handmade (pieced, appliqued, embroidered & quilted); quilt never used; a family treasure, but it's time for it to be treasured by another family. $575.00

5190393 – FLOWER GARDEN; 78" x 98"; white, hunter green plus a variety of colors w/yellow centers; cotton; made in Illinois in 1992; machine pieced, hand quilted; polyester batting; made w/all new materials. $310.00

6190393 – FARMER'S DAUGHTER; 78" x 93"; rose & blue; poly/cotton broadcloth, muslin backing; made in Arkansas in 1989; machine pieced, hand quilted; poly batt; quilt never used. $230.00

7190393 – SPRING FLOWERS; 67" x 103"; all solid colors, red tulips, gold centers, medium teal green leaves, pure white background; 100% cottons; made in Virginia in 1992; machine pieced, hand appliqued stems, hand quilted; polyester batting; heavily quilted with 6 & 10 row cables; cabled pillow tuck area, double bias bound w/mitered corners; totally reversible as backing is also white. $397.00

115

1010693

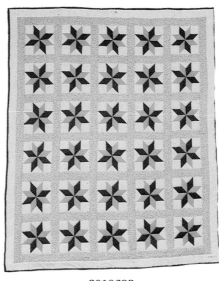

2010693

3010693

4010693

5010693

6010693

7010693

1010693 – LONE STAR; 84" x 84"; red, green, yellow w/white background; all cotton on front, back is off-white homespun; made in North Carolina c.1870-1885; hand pieced & quilted in double diamond grid; professional conserved; excellent condition. $1150.00

2010693 – 8 POINTED STAR; 83" x 98"; blue & mauve w/white background; cotton/polyester; made in Missouri recently; machine pieced, hand quilted; polyester batting. $345.00

3010693 – LANCASTER ROSE; 93" x 108"; light cream off-white backing & background, peach (plain & print) flowers, light green micropot leaves; 100% cotton; made in Michigan in 1991; all handmade (applique, quilting, binding & setting together); polyester batting. $575.00

4010693 – STRIP & TRIANGLE QUILT; 91" x 103"; backing is peach, top is strips of rose, green, peach & blue for half the block, the other half is a triangle of a print of the same colors; cotton; made in Pennsylvania in 1992; machine pieced, hand quilted; polyester batting. $575.00

5010693 – PENNSYLVANIA STATE STAR; 92" x 98"; blue w/white background; cotton/polyester; recently made in Missouri; machine pieced, hand quilted; polyester batting. $402.00

6010693 – DOUBLE DUTCH CHAIN; 67" x 77"; yellow, brown, blues; cotton & cotton/polyester; made in New Mexico in 1992; machine pieced & quilted; Fairfield traditional batting. $259.00

7010693 – WEDDING RING; 87" x 110"; black w/rose & green on off-white background; all cotton; made in Kansas in 1991; machine pieced, hand quilted; polyester batting; double binding; the off-white is a beige-on-beige w/a little flower design. $397.00

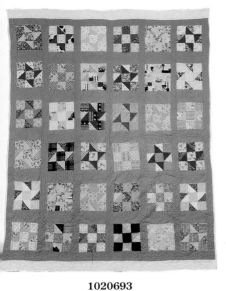

1020693

2020693

3020693

4020693

5020693

6020693

1020693 – 9 PATCH BLOCK; 84" x 100"; country blue w/multicolored & plain blocks, white border; cotton and cotton/polyester blend fabrics; made in Iowa in 1985; machine pieced, hand quilted; traditional Mountain Mist batting; excellent condition (top from the 1960's w/many colors). $253.00

2020693 – PINWHEEL; 88" x 101"; dark & medium blue prints w/white background; cotton/polyester; made in Missouri in 1992; machine pieced, hand quilted; polyester batting. $402.00

3020693 – COUNTRY BLOSSOMS; 100" x 111"; white background, strips of peach chintz, persian rose; 100% cotton; made in Utah in 1993; machine pieced, hand quilted & embroidered; Dacron™ batting (Taylor); embroidered in medium & dark jewel toned colors; features a basket of flowers in wicker brown. $978.00

4020693 – ALABAMA STATE STAR; 92" x 97"; black & white prints w/white background; cotton/polyester; made in Missouri in 1992; machine pieced, hand quilted; polyester batting. $402.00

5020693 – PROSPERITY BLOCKED; 35" x 35"; dusty green, off-white, multicolored; cotton; made in North Dakota in 1992; machine pieced, hand quilted; won a red ribbon at state fair; "greed, not concern for ecology truly blocks prosperity." $200.00

6020693 – DIAMONDS; 80" x 92"; multicolored print, off-white solid, broadcloth; mostly print cotton fabric, some calico print; made in Tennessee in 1989; hand pieced & quilted; polyester batting, bleached sheeting. $345.00

7020693 – AMISH SHADOW; 92" x 92"; black, purple, green & blue; cottons; made in Illinois in 1992; machine pieced & quilted; polyester batting. $230.00

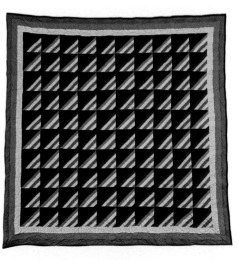

7020693

1030693

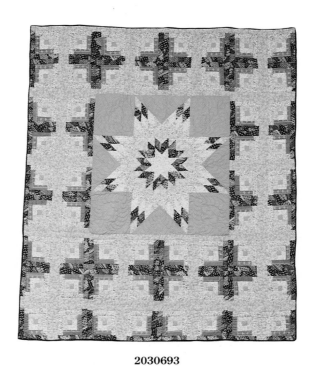

2030693

3030693

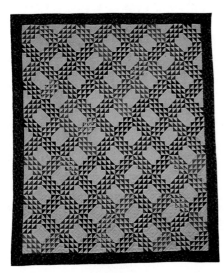

4030693

5030693

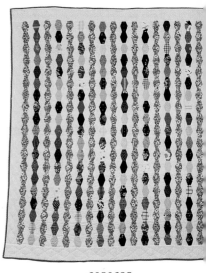

6030693

7030693

1030693 – SAILBOAT; 42" x 55"; white, blue & yellow; cotton; made in New York in 1992; machine pieced, hand quilted; polyester batting. $144.00

2030693 – PRAIRIE STAR - LOG CABIN; 88" x 100"; blues & pinks; polyester/cotton blends; made Indiana in 1991; machine pieced, hand quilted; polyfil extra loft batting; an original design using star & cab blocks. $397.00

3030693 – CRAZY QUILT; 36" x 59"; scraps of all colors; cotton & cotton/polyester blends; made North Carolina in 1992; machine pieced & tied; rectangular blocks, rust backing; polyester batting. $86.00

4030693 – OCEAN WAVES; 88" x 103"; blue, red, blacks w/sandy brown printed background; all cotton made in Indiana in 1992; machine pieced, hand quilted; 120 8" squares, 5" border w/matching binding; pol ester batting. $805.00

5030693 – BRIDAL WREATH APPLIQUE; 93" x 106"; multicolored applique w/off-white background cotton & cotton/polyester blends; made in California in 1984; hand appliqued & quilted; polyester batting intricately hand quilted. $690.00

6030693 – TILE QUILT; 83" x 96"; red the main color w/white background and backing; cotton and co ton/polyester; made in Arkansas in 1991; hand pieced & quilted; polyester batting; various prints used; re binding. $259.00

7030693 – STORM AT SEA; 94" x 110"; dark or navy blue on a lighter blue; broadcloth 50/5 cotton/polyester; made in Delaware in 1991; machine pieced, hand quilted & hand bound; polyester battin $573.00

118

1040693

2040693

3040693

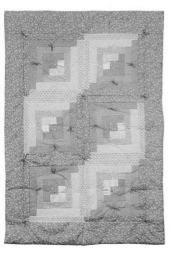

4040693

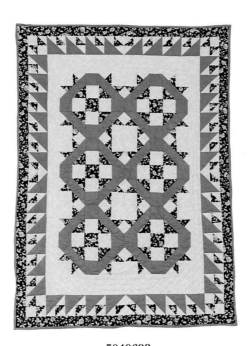

5040693

6040693

1040693 – TRIP AROUND THE WORLD; 61" x 87"; dusty pink, unbleached muslin backing; 100% pre-washed cotton fabrics; made in Colorado in 1992; machine pieced, hand tied in every corner; extra loft batting. $201.00

2040693 – LOG CABIN; 44" x 44"; pastel blues, pinks, lavenders w/beige border; 100% cotton; made in Georgia in 1991; machine pieced, hand quilted; polyester batting; sleeve for hanging. $172.00

3040693 – DIAGONAL TRIANGLES; 82" x 107"; traditional Amish quilt in striking, bold Amish colors; all prewashed cotton; made in Illinois in 1993; intricately hand quilted, machine pieced; Hobbs bonded black batting. $690.00

4040693 – LOG CABIN; 36" x 52"; peach & white florals; cotton & cotton/polyester blends; made in Oregon in 1992; machine pieced, hand tied; polyester batting; use as baby quilt or wallhanging; matching fabric on back. $50.00

5040693 – DAVID & GOLIATH; 31" x 42" (correct size); navy, rose, off-white; cotton & polished cottons; made in Minnesota in 1993; machine pieced, hand quilted; polyester batting. $172.00

6040693 – HIDDEN WELLS; 60" x 90"; peach & tan; cottons; made in Pennsylvania in 1991; hand quilted; polyester batting. $282.00

7040693 – MAPLE LEAF; 42" x 42"; contemporary scrap colors on cream background; 100% cotton prewashed; made in Louisiana in 1993; machine pieced & quilted in diagonal grid w/ cotton thread; Hobbs Heirloom cotton batting; double binding. $288.00

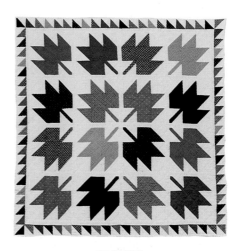

7040693

1050693

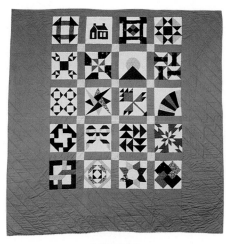

2050693

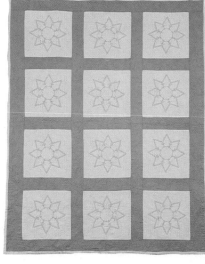

3050693

4050693

5050693

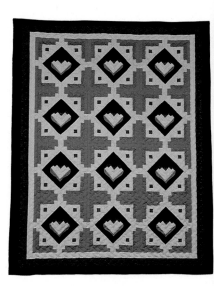

6050693

7050693

1050693 – TULIP SURROUND; 90" x 103"; light greens for background, darker greens, lavender & deep purple in borders, multicolored medallion; 100% cotton; made in Virginia in 1991; machine pieced border, hand quilted & appliqued; double bias binding; polyester batting; lots of quilting in this one. $1380.00

2050693 – SAMPLER; 96" x 94"; blue & off-white; made in Wisconsin recently; machine pieced & quilted; cotton batting. $402.00

3050693 – CROSS STITCH STAR; 69" x 85"; gold & white top reverses to white back; cotton; made c.1930 in Missouri, maker unknown; hand pieced & quilted, white squares embroidered w/gold thread; cotton batting; quilted in leaf & vine design; this quilt was a wedding gift. $431.00

4050693 – BEAR PAW; 80" x 96"; dark red w/a background fabric of cream & red/rose leaves; cotton/polyester blend fabrics used; made in Connecticut in 1991-92; machine pieced, hand quilted w/dark red thread, plain blocks have quilted hearts; double bias binding; polyester batting, white backing. $345.00

5050693 – BETTY BOOP; 55" x 75"; mauve & cream color; cotton & polyester blends; made in Kentucky in 1992; machine pieced, hand painted; made w/new fabrics. $230.00

6050693 – LOG CABIN HEART; 86" x 106"; Amish light & dark colors; light – blue, teal, peach, violet; dark – black, purple, burgundy, green, navy; cotton & cotton blends; made in Indiana in 1993; machine pieced & quilted; polyester batting; the quilt is reversible. $259.00

7050693 – FOX & GEESE; 67" x 81"; gold & red on muslin; 100% cotton; unknown maker c.1910 in Tennessee; hand pieced & quilted; cotton batting; original binding (badly frayed) has been replaced, but could be removed, a few patches have been repaired; quilted in both white & gray/black thread; an interesting old quilt. $201.00

120

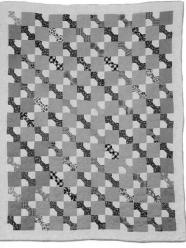

1060693

2060693

3060693

4060693

5060693

6060693

1060693 – BOW TIE; 74" x 88"; prints on blue background; cotton fabrics; history of this old quilt is unknown; machine pieced, hand quilted; unbleached lining. $230.00

2060693 – ROSEVILLE USA; 28" x 47"; colonial blue, navy, rose shades, forest green, dark brown; cotton; made in Pennsylvania in 1992; hand quilted; architectural & scenic details. $155.00

3060693 – LONE OR TEXAS STAR; 32" x 32"; maroon background & border, off-white, tan & peachy brown inside, mitered border fabric; all cotton; made in Pennsylvania in 1991; machine pieced, hand quilted; cotton batting; sleeve for hanging; used as a teacher's example on Lone Star construction. $144.00

4060693 – STAR WHEEL; 84" x 98"; blue & red stars and triangles on white background; cotton; made in Michigan in 1972; machine pieced, hand quilted w/outline stitch around each piece & floral design between each wheel; one small stain on back of quilt. $397.00

5060693 – LOG CABIN; 101" x 127"; light prints w/few pastels on one side of block, blacks & fully saturated colors on the other; 100% cottons & cotton blends; made in Utah in 1992; 1" finished logs, machine pieced, hand quilted on every log; non-bonded Morning Glory batting. $1061.00

6060693 – NOT NAMED; 72" x 96"; off-white; polyester & cotton; made in Pennsylvania in 1992; hand quilted; batting Dacron™/polyester. $345.00

7060693 – LOG CABIN; 74" x 88"; tan & yellow prints, solid yellow binding; cotton; made in Alabama in 1987; machine pieced, hand quilted on each side of seam; polyester batting; yellow sheet for lining. $259.00

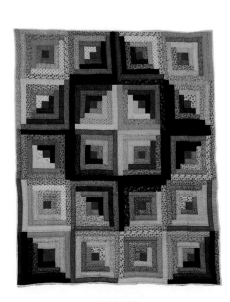

7060693

1070693

2070693

3070693

4070693

5070693

6070693

7070693

1070693 – CHERRY RIPE; 78" x 92"; red, green, lavender, white background; cotton; made in Missouri in 1934; hand pieced, quilted & appliqued; cotton batting, Stearns & Foster pattern; won blue ribbons at state fairs in Missouri & California. $575.00

2070693 – CHRISTMAS SAMPLER; 36" x 36"; cream background w/dark red & green prints & solids; 100% cotton; made in Florida in 1990; hand pieced & quilted; Mountain Mist Light batting; teacher's example on border prints. $144.00

3070693 – GRANDMOTHER'S FLOWER GARDEN; 90" x 111"; off-white background w/multi harmonizing plain-colored flowers accented w/blue path; mostly 100% cotton w/some cotton/poly blends; made in Utah in 1992; hand pieced & quilted; Dacron™ batting; quilted around each hexagon; pale blue cotton blend back; lots of quilting. $978.00

4070693 – TEDDY BEAR; 35" x 45"; yellow, brown, multicolored Teddy Bear print; 100% cotton; made in Wisconsin in 1993; hand & machine pieced & quilted, hand embroidered & appliqued; colors suited for boy or girl; polyester batting. $70.00

5070693 – GIANT DAHLIA; 94" x 117"; white back, blue, light to dark shades of prints; cotton/polyester; made in Illinois in 1992; machine pieced, hand quilted; polyester batting. $247.00

6070693 – MARY HAD A LITTLE LAMB; 36" x 51"; soft green & peach; 65/35 poly/cotton broadcloth; made in Illinois in 1990; machine pieced, hand quilted; polyester batting; never used. $86.00

7070693 – BASKET GARDEN; 66" x 84"; medium & light green w/off-white background; 100% cotton top except for a few applique patches, 50/50 blend backing; made in Virginia in 1991; hand pieced, appliqued & quilted; patterns mostly taken from Basket Garden by Mary Hickey; polyester batting. $288.00

1080693

2080693

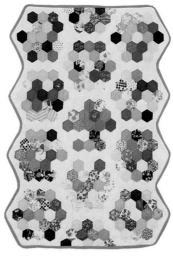

3080693

4080693

5080693

6080693

1080693 – ALPHABET QUILT; 33" x 39"; black, black print of tiny roses in border, multicolored-soft shades, blues, roses, greens, etc. in letters; machine pieced & appliqued, hand quilted by Amish; polyester batting; Williamsburg blue thread used to satin stitch appliques; backed w/solid black cotton, black quilting thread. $115.00

2080693 – IRISH CHAIN; 85" x 96"; blue & black; 100% cotton; maker of antique top unknown; quilt made in Nebraska in 1992; machine & hand pieced, hand quilted; Mountain Mist batting; coordinated backing. $402.00

3080693 – COLONIAL GARDEN; 38" x 52"; variegated prints & mint green; cotton & cotton/polyester blends; made in Kentucky in 1990; hand pieced & quilted; green lining; polyester batting; crib quilt or wall decor. $55.00

4080693 – TUNNEL OF LOVE; 65" x 87"; blue, ecru & maroon; cotton/polyester blend fabrics; made in Nebraska in 1993; machine pieced & quilted; polyfil batting; muslin backing. $144.00

5080693 – JACOB'S LADDER; 80" x 95"; blocks are flower print of rose, orchid & light green w/solid rose, the background is white, border is same solid rose; cotton/polyester blend; made in Missouri in 1993; machine pieced & quilted; polyester batting. $201.00

6080693 – SUNSHINE & SHADOW - IRISH CHAIN; 90" x 106"; dark red to white; broadcloth; made in 1992 in Pennsylvania; machine pieced, hand quilted; polyester batting; lots of fine hand quilting; six shades of red to white. $518.00

7080693 – DOUBLE WEDDING RING; 96" x 96"; off-white background, multicolored prints; top is machine pieced, hand quilted; quilt completed in Minnesota in 1992 (top is older); typical patchwork quilt w/ assorted prints & solids & muslins; polyester batting; natural color bias binding. $268.00

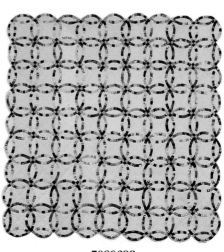

7080693

123

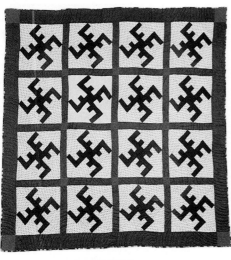

1090693

2090693

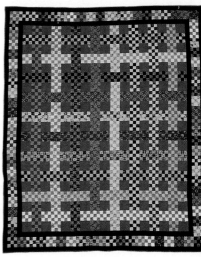

3090693

4090693

5090693

6090693

7090693

1090693 – LETTER F OR FLORA'S FAVORITE; 74" x 74"; red, green & blue. This quilt was made shortly after the Civil War by Lila Land Chun, Bartow, GA.; heavy cotton batt; excellent condition; a rare find. $494.00

2090693 – JOY - NOEL TREE; 34" x 34"; red & green pin dots, Christmas prints, white background; made in Pennsylvania in 1990; machine pieced, hand quilted & appliqued; Mountain Mist Quilt-Light batting; holiday motifs outline quilted. $86.00

3090693 – NINE-PATCH INTERWEAVE; 91" x 106"; red, multi-earth tones; 100% cotton; made in North Carolina in 1992; machine pieced, free-motion machine quilted; low-loft polyester batting; pattern gives look of interweaving ribbons. $402.00

4090693 – GOD'S PROMISE; 84" x 84"; blue, red, maroon, orange, green & yellow; cotton/polyester blends; made in Georgia in 1991; machine pieced, hand quilted; low-loft batting; adapted from John Flynn's King's Covenant and modified; ribbon winner in Home Federal's show in Gainesville, FL in 1991. $748.00

5090693 – ENCIRCLED TULIP; 89" x 104"; burgundy w/shades of rose & pink with white; all cotton; made in Kansas in 1992; machine pieced, hand quilted & appliqued; polyester batting, poly/cotton lining; double bias. $397.00

6090693 – ALBUM; 37" x 37"; multicolored prints w/peach print background; burgundy print border; cotton & cotton blends; made in Colorado in 1990; machine pieced, hand quilted; polyester batting, red plaid flannel back. $115.00

7090693 – VIRGINIA REEL; 58" x 74"; shades of spring greens w/hyacinth purples & pinks; 100% cotton; made in California in 1993; machine pieced & quilted; Cotton Classic batting; machine quilting done in curved snail pattern to "put a spin" on whirling figures of the Virginia Reel block. $288.00

124

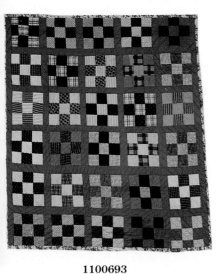

1100693

2100693

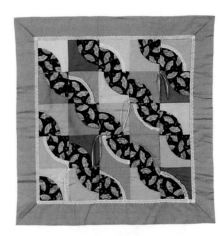

3100693

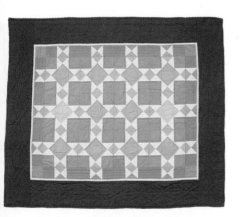

4100693

5100693

6100693

1100693 – ANTIQUE NINE PATCH IN GREEN SASHES; 67" x 78"; indigo, white plaids & stripes, pink, orange, brown & black prints & calicoes; cottons and cretonne backing; unknown maker c.1890 in Iowa; machine pieced, hand quilted; most of the fabrics on the top are from shirtings; no torn or stained areas; quilting stitches are large, batting is thick; cretonne backing has at least 8 different scenes from the late 1800's. $288.00

2100693 – BRAIDED HEARTS; 36" x 45"; red, black & off-white; 100% cotton; made in Washington in 1992; machine pieced & quilted; braided hearts are topped by red ribbon bows; hanging sleeve at top. $70.00

3100693 – GEORGIA PEACH; 76" x 91"; off-white, mauve, blue; 100% cotton; made in Oklahoma in 1992; machine pieced & hand quilted by one person; won Grand Champion at county fair in 1992. $805.00

4100693 – EVENING STAR; 39" x 47"; shades of blue, off-white, green, blue border; 100% cotton; made in Georgia in 1992; machine pieced, hand quilted; polyester batting; sleeve for hanging. $92.00

5100693 – BLUEBIRDS FOR HAPPINESS; 92" x 102"; blue print birds, blue solid, white & natural muslin pieces & border; permapress cottons; made in California in 1993; blocks are hand pieced, straight seams machine made, hand quilted; Mountain Mist batting; bluebirds form a 6-point star; backing is miniature blue rosebuds. $489.00

6100693 – FANS; 28" x 28"; mauves, greens, black; 100% cotton; made in Indiana in 1991; hand appliqued & quilted, machine pieced; Mountain Mist Quilt Light batting; antique handmade lace, ribbons & pearls. $104.00

7100693 – FAN PATTERN; 84" x 96"; mauve, pale pink & cranberry - fans are multicolored; cotton; made in Arkansas in 1990; machine pieced & quilted (quilting pattern called "cloud"; polyfil batting, backing is 100% cotton in very tiny blue pattern VIP & tiny peach pattern; reversible quilt; quilt is new but has been washed. $115.00

7100693

1110693

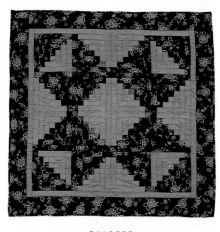

2110693

3110693

4110693

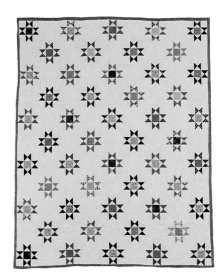

5110693

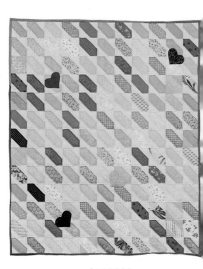

6110693

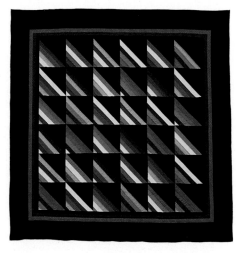

7110693

1110693 – DRESDEN PLATE; 80" x 96"; country blue w/light cream background; all cotton top wit[h] cotton/poly blend back; made in Kansas in 1993; machine pieced, hand quilted; mitered corners, doub[le] binding; Hobbs polyester batting. $368.00

2110693 – STAR; 38" x 38"; mauve, black print w/metallic gold, blue, green & purple; cotton/poly[-] ester blends; made in Nebraska in 1992; machine pieced, hand quilted; polyfil batting; sleeve on back fo[r] hanging. $83.00

3110693 – STARS OVER FLORIDA; 82" x 100"; multicolored calico prints in country colors & musli[n] all 100% prewashed cotton; made in Illinois in 1993; machine pieced, hand quilted; soft blue paisley back[;] quilted w/hearts in corners. $575.00

4110693 – COLORADO LOG CABIN; 70" x 85"; shades of baby blue to navy w/bright blue stars; co[t-] ton; made in Michigan in 1991; machine pieced, hand quilted; Mountain Mist polyester batting; prewashe[d] fabrics, borders crosshatched quilted. $230.00

5110693 – OHIO STAR; 84" x 101"; muslin background w/rose & blue stars; 100% cotton fabrics[;] made in California in 1993; machine pieced, hand quilted; cotton batting. $345.00

6110693 – INDIAN HATCHET; 58" x 69"; pale yellow w/pinks, blues and green calicoes-prints &[solids; 100% cotton top, cotton/poly blend back; made in California in 1991; machine pieced, han[d] appliqued hearts, hand quilted; extra loft batting; back is white w/peach calico print; double fold bias bin[d-] ing. $402.00

7110693 – ROMAN STRIPE WALL QUILT; 56" x 56"; solid black background, stripes of solid re[d,] purple, royal blue, yellow, copper & taupe; all cotton fabrics; made in Illinois in 1991; machine pieced[;] close hand quilting, feather design quilted in border; Hobbs dark batting, quilted w/black thread; ready t[o] hang for wall display. $499.00

126

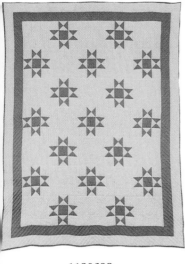

1120693

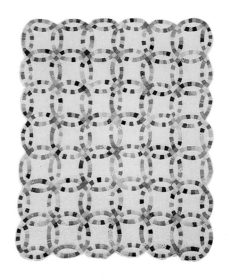

2120693

3120693

4120693

5120693

6120693

1120693 – OHIO STAR; 77" x 100"; blue & white; cotton; made in Texas in 1992; machine pieced, hand quilted; quilted w/feather wreath border; Mountain Mist batting $345.00

2120693 – APPLIQUED WREATH; 30" x 30"; off-white background, navy, pink & green flowers, leaves & borders; cotton & cotton/polyester blends; made in North Carolina in 1988; hand appliqued & quilted; polyester batting; floral applique wreath. $115.00

3120693 – DOUBLE WEDDING RING; 79" x 94"; purple w/white background; cotton/polyester blend fabrics; made in Missouri in 1991; machine pieced, hand quilted. $288.00

4120693 – BORROW PETER TO PAY PAUL; 62" x 86"; orange & white; cotton; made in Missouri in 1931; hand pieced, hand quilted; cotton batting; given as a wedding gift in 1940 and kept as family heirloom – never used! $575.00

5120693 – GIANT DAHLIA; 91" x 110"; pink, blue, gray w/rose back; cotton/polyester; made in Illinois in 1992; machine pieced, hand quilted; polyester batting. $247.00

6120693 – SOUTH WEST TRIP AROUND THE WORLD; 44" x 62"; cream, blue, green, wine, mauve & tan; 100% cottons; made in Indiana in 1991; machine pieced, hand quilted; polyester batting; the basket weave border original design of quiltmaker. $172.00

7120693 – OHIO ROSE; 76" x 91"; white, pink & green; cotton and cotton/polyester (the green & lining is blend); made in Ohio in 1988; hand appliqued & quilted; polyester batting. $575.00

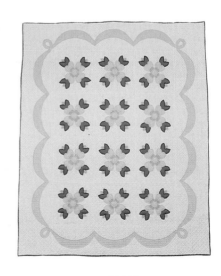

7120693

❧ American Quilter's Society ❧
dedicated to publishing books for today's quilters